The History Handbook

Second Edition

Carol Berkin

Baruch College,
City University of New York

Betty S. Anderson

Boston University

WADSWORTH
CENGAGE Learning™

Australia • Brazil • Japan • Korea • Mexico • Singapore • Spain • United Kingdom • United States

The History Handbook, Second Edition
Carol Berkin

Senior Publisher:
Suzanne Jeans

Senior Sponsoring Editor:
Ann West

Assistant Editor:
Megan Chrisman

Editorial Assistant:
Patrick Roach

Senior Media Editor:
Lisa Ciccolo

Senior Marketing Manager:
Katherine Bates

Marketing Coordinator:
Lorreen Pelletier

Marketing Communications
Manager: Caitlin Green

Content Project Management:
PreMediaGlobal

Senior Art Director:
Cate Rickard Barr

Print Buyer:
Betsy Donaghey

Senior Rights Acquisition
Specialist, Text: Katie Huha

Senior Image Rights Specialist:
Jennifer Meyer Dare

Compositor: PreMediaGlobal

Cover Designer: © Wing-ip
Ngan, Ink design, Inc.

Cover Image: "Spinning Silk"
from *Precetti dell'Arte della Seta'*
(Rules of the Silk Guild),
Biblioteca Medicea-
Laurenziana, Florence.
Courtesy of The Bridgeman
Art Library International Ltd.

For product information and technology assistance, contact us at
Cengage Learning Customer & Sales Support, 1-800-354-9706

For permission to use material from this text or product,
submit all requests online at **www.cengage.com/permissions**
Further permissions questions can be emailed to
permissionrequest@cengage.com

Library of Congress Control Number: 2010933298

ISBN-13: 978-0-495-90676-6

ISBN-10: 0-495-90676-X

Wadsworth
20 Channel Center Street
Boston, MA 02210
USA

Cengage Learning is a leading provider of customized learning solutions with office locations around the globe, including Singapore, the United Kingdom, Australia, Mexico, Brazil and Japan. Locate your local office at **www.cengage.com/global**

Cengage Learning products are represented in Canada by Nelson Education, Ltd.

For your course and learning solutions, visit
www.cengage.com

Purchase any of our products at your local college store or at our preferred online store **www.cengagebrain.com**

Printed in the United States of America
1 2 3 4 5 6 7 14 13 12 11 10

907.1
BER

Contents

36.95

Preface

The authors of this *Handbook* still remember their freshman history class with a combination of horror and humor. We both recall frantically underlining almost every sentence in the textbook. We remember the panic we felt when a professor handed out instructions for the first written assignment as well as our sweaty palms when we had to take our first in-class exam. Worst of all, perhaps, were our first stumbling efforts at doing historical research.

Watching our students go through the same traumas we did semester after semester, we wondered: Was this an inevitable rite of passage every student must endure? Did every student have to learn the hard way, by trial and error, mistake and regret? Was it really impossible for a freshman to enjoy a history course and do well in it? Our answer to all these questions was a resounding "No." And this is why we sat down to write *The History Handbook.*

Our basic premise is simple: Success in a history class is within the reach of every student. But like all specialized disciplines, history has its tricks of the trade, and mastering them is the key to that success. Thus, the *History Handbook* is, above all, a collection of practical suggestions on everything from how to tackle a textbook and study for an exam to how to turn the Internet into an effective research tool. The *Handbook* is not a theoretical collection of ideas; it is a concrete tool, providing clear definitions and helpful examples on every topic. Although the *Handbook* is primarily a no-nonsense guide to the skills you'll need in a history course, it also introduces you to the type of questions historians ask and the variety of sources they turn to for answers to those questions. It is a guide both to how to "do" history and how to do well in a history class.

One of our main goals was to make *The History Handbook* genuinely accessible to all students. Realizing that you're often in a hurry to find specific help on a particular topic, we open each chapter with a bulleted list of all the topics being covered within it and end each chapter with a brief "Recap," providing similar content information. These features guarantee that you won't have to read through the entire *Handbook* to find the solution to that one particular—and urgent—problem. Throughout the *Handbook*, you'll see a special feature called "Helping Hand." In these "Helping Hand" segments, we level with you. We give you the teacher's point of view on what is happening in the classroom and remind you that professors are people too. We also offer sage and sensible advice on developing good study habits. Much of what we say in the "Helping Hand" features may sound familiar—don't try to cram the night before the exam! Don't leave the research for a paper to the last minute! Don't fall behind in your assigned readings! But remember—just because you've heard it before doesn't mean it isn't excellent advice. Finally, we've added a Glossary so that even new information isn't mysterious.

The companion student website takes advantage of the breadth of resources available to you on the World Wide Web. This site includes Web activities for each chapter, updated for use with the second edition, as well as interactive maps, which are new to this edition. You can link to select websites to get help in researching history topics, access online versions of a variety of style guides, and more. The site also features a Glossary of key terms.

What skills do we think are essential for success in a history course? The answer can be found by looking closely at the table of contents. The basic "how tos" of taking notes in class, getting the most out of lectures and class discussions, tackling the textbook effectively, using technology effectively for research and writing, and studying for a variety of exam types are laid out in Chapters 1 through 3. Because interpreting and understanding maps is an important part of a history course, we've included a whole chapter on how maps can help you understand history. And, because you will have to learn to recognize the difference between primary sources, secondary sources, and works of fiction as well as learn how to use each of these types of works in your history course, we've included a chapter on that subject as well. Since most history classes require you to write papers, we've devoted Chapters 6 through 8 to every aspect of the writing process, from picking a topic to conducting research to organizing an essay. These chapters contain useful suggestions on using both the library and the Web. In Chapter 9, we offer a guide to oral rather than written projects such as debates or role playing. Because most colleges have developed guidelines against plagiarism, we've also included two chapters on this form of intellectual theft, carefully defining plagiarism and explaining how to cite the sources you use appropriately. We've also included a chapter on those rules of grammar that help you communicate your ideas to others. The final chapter of the *Handbook*, "Are There Any Other Tips I Should Know?" allows us to share a variety of other valuable tips that come from years of being both students and professors ourselves.

Because technology has become a critical part of the learning process, we've revisited every chapter of the book in this new edition and added tips for the best use of new technologies from PowerPoint® to Facebook. We have also expanded and updated Chapter 13, on the opportunities and challenges of the online classroom.

You've probably noticed that we haven't attempted to provide a long defense of history or its importance, for we believe that you'll recognize the value of history as you become involved in its study. Instead, *The History Handbook* provides a guide to developing the skills you need to succeed in a college history class. Once those skills are acquired, our hope is that you'll be able to relax and join in some of the fun.

Carol Berkin would like to give special thanks to Roberta McCutcheon, head of the history department at Trevor Day School in New York City, and Angelo Angelis, Assistant Professor of History at Hunter College, who both read drafts of the manuscript and offered sage advice based on their years of teaching. Both authors are also grateful to the following instructors, who read and criticized the manuscript throughout its development:

Peter K. Bacon, U.S. Military Academy at West Point
Emerson W. Baker, Salem State College
Linda Bregstein, Mercer County Community College
Jerry Cooper, University of Missouri, St. Louis
Anthony J. Heideman, U.S. Naval Academy
Randolph Hollingsworth, University of Kentucky
Toren Hudson, South Texas Community College
Earl F. Mulderink III, Southern Utah University
William H. Mulligan, Jr., Murray State University
Patrick M. Patterson, Honolulu Community College
Alice E. Reagan, Northern Virginia Community College, Woodbridge
Patrick D. Reagan, Tennessee Technological University
Denise S. Spooner, California State University, Northridge
Janet A.Thompson, Tallahassee Community College
Louise Blakeney Williams, Central Connecticut State University
Kathleen Xidis, Johnson County Community College

We would also like to thank Charles Forcey for his contribution to this edition.

C.B.
B.S.A.

The History Handbook

Introduction

What Is History and Why Is It Important?

Here you are, in your first college history class, and you might be wondering: What can history do that will help me in my college career—and afterward? We're glad you asked.

First, the study of history sharpens your reading and your writing skills. Many historians are master storytellers and their books are good examples of how to narrate a tale, describe an event, and vividly capture the character of a person so that the reader feels they know that person intimately. These are skills that you will be called on to demonstrate in most of your other courses in college. They are also skills we all wish we had worked on when we are trying to make conversation at a party, sell a product to potential buyers, or write an evaluation of a colleague or employee. Other historians have penetrating, focused minds; they carry us, step by step, through a process of analysis that shows us how a muddle of apparently unconnected information actually has a logical thread. Like good detectives, they demonstrate how to gather clues, create the connections among them, and distinguish cause and consequence from accident and coincidence. Who doesn't want to be more like Sherlock Holmes when they are analyzing stocks, putting together a legal defense, weeding out too much information from the Internet, or even figuring out who stole cookies from the cookie jar? There is no way around it: history books provide models for communicating, analyzing, and organizing ideas and information. This is why many of the best lawyers, judges, corporate executives, and teachers majored in history in college.

Second, doing history yourself—writing book reviews, producing research papers, giving oral reports in class, and writing an essay that compares one event to another or explains why something happened and what results it produced—allows you to test and hone these skills for yourself. Knowing where to find information, how to evaluate it, and how to discern the connections among many pieces of information are essential talents in this era of information revolutions and the Internet. They are also talents that will serve you well as long as you are a person who wants to make independent judgments about important issues in your personal and professional life.

Finally, history is just plain fun—and even the most serious and ambitious college students need some fun. Where else can you find so many zany or heroic characters? Open any history book and you will find con men and philosophers, women's rights advocates and dance hall girls, kings, queens, revolutionaries, and paupers who became millionaires, plus an endless assortment of assassins, murderers, madmen, and poets. Where else is there so much drama and excitement? For sheer nail-biting, edge-of-your-seat tension, what can compete with the fall of Rome, the decision to drop the atomic bomb, the voyages of Christopher Columbus, or the first humans landing on the moon? Not even the most ambitious movie director can produce the rise and fall of so many nations, bloody battles and secret peace negotiations, inventions, discoveries, horrifying acts of cruelty, and crusades for human rights. Murder, mayhem, romance—history has them all, and more.

Interested? Read on. *The History Handbook* will provide you with a step-by-step guide to developing all the skills you need to succeed in your first college history class. It will allow you to relax, and share in some of the fun.

The History Handbook is a straightforward "how-to" book designed for speedy reference. It is organized so that you can quickly find help for the problem you are facing. Each chapter begins with a preview of what will be covered, called Tips in This Chapter. Throughout each chapter you will see a feature called Helping Hand, in which the authors modestly share their experience and wisdom drawn from many years as students themselves and as professors. At the end of every chapter, you will find a brief section called Recap, which sums up the main topics that the chapter has covered.

Now, you should be ready to begin.

*H*ow Can I Succeed in My History Class?

- *What will help me most?*
- *How many notes should I take during the lecture?*
- *Why are class discussions important?*
- *Can I ask the professor for help?*

TIPS IN THIS CHAPTER

- Taking notes in class
- Getting the most from classroom discussions
- Getting help from the professor
- Being a responsible student

What Will Help Me Most?

The following three suggestions may seem obvious, but they are critical nevertheless.

First, go to class. Professors are frustrated when students don't come to class and then arrive at the end of the semester to complain about the heavy workload or ask for an extension. Professors will generally be more responsive to students they know and see on a regular basis.

Second, go to class prepared to participate. Most professors consider classroom participation important. To be part of any class discussion, you need to be caught up on the reading assignments. It will also help if you jot down some questions or observations about the readings or the material covered in the last lecture or class discussion. If you are a naturally shy person, arriving with notes on the reading and a provocative question or two will help you jump into the discussion. Take advantage of online course communication tools like discussion boards to make clear, coherent, and provocative arguments that might otherwise be hard to think up on the spot during regular classroom discussions. Remember, never to try to score points with your professor by making fun of another student's comments. Constructive criticism will be welcome; personal attacks on a classmate will not.

Third, keep up with the work. Don't leave everything until the night before the paper is due or the exam is scheduled. Don't fool yourself into believing the old clichés of "I do better when I'm under pressure" or "I can't write a paper until the night before it's due." If you try to cram at the last moment, you will not do well. Well-written papers don't fly out of the computer printer in the middle of the night. You need to attend class regularly, complete all the readings and assignments, and review all of your notes regularly. Check the course website regularly for announcements, review any grade book sections for missing homework or quizzes, and take advantage of lecture notes, PowerPoint® slides, videos, or podcasts that might help you review or catch up on any missed classes.

How Many Notes Should I Take During the Lecture?

Unless you have mastered shorthand or are a speed typist, you cannot hope to take down everything your professor or your classmates say. While you are furiously scribbling down or typing the professor's first sentence, you are probably missing something important that he or she is saying in the second sentence. Is it hopeless? Not if you think before you write. Try following these six steps if you're attending a class lecture.

☞ *HELPING HAND*   Should I bring my laptop, tablet, or recorder? Many students bring a portable computer, recording device, or both into classrooms. Although many of you can type faster than you can write by hand, don't underestimate the memory and learning connections between hearing, seeing, and handwriting a succinct summary of your professor's points. With attention, both manual and electronic methods can result in excellent notes and good information recall, but laptop users may be tempted to try to produce a verbatim transcript with little or no mental engagement. Distractions from Internet-connected laptops, personal digital assistants, and phones are also becoming a classroom epidemic, leading to outright bans of these otherwise useful devices at some schools. Be intentional about the tools and gadgets you bring into the class, and be willing to drop back to tried-and-true pen and paper if you feel any of your gadgets might be distracting you. If other students' web surfing, text messaging, or even headphone use is making it hard to concentrate, move closer to the front of the class and, confidentially, share the experience with the professor so he or she can clarify the classroom policies on electronic devices.

First, if the professor puts an outline for the day's topic on the board, copy it down immediately. (You might even want to get into the habit of arriving early so that you can transfer the outline into your notebook before the lecture begins.) If the professor hands out an outline or posts it on the website, make sure you add it to your notebook immediately.

☞ *HELPING HAND*   Make the most of the professor's outline by adding
to it. Fill in examples taken from the lecture, class discussion, and/or
the assigned reading that illustrate the main points on that outline.
Add your own informed comments and questions. Add relevant
dates and names. Define terms used on the outline.

Second, if the professor begins the lecture with a series of questions
or interpretive statements to be answered or proven during the course
of the lecture, use them as the heading for the day's notes. If you are
lucky, the professor will end the day's lecture with a summary of what
was covered. If you add this summary to your notes, you will have produced the same format as a textbook chapter.

☞ *HELPING HAND*   Let the professor be your note-taking guide.
If her opening question is "What were the main causes of the
French Revolution?" then don't take elaborate notes on the
execution of Queen Marie Antoinette (even if the gory details are
exciting).

Third, listen carefully as the professor develops the day's theme
or topic. He or she will probably provide several examples for each
point along the way. Don't try to copy all of these examples down.
Instead, choose one or two examples that you feel illustrate the point
best for you.

Fourth, listen closely to any questions asked by classmates during or
after the lecture. Record the question and the response if you feel both
clarify an issue for you.

Fifth, do you have a question? Is there something you aren't sure
you understood or something you are especially curious about that
the professor did not cover? Ask—and then record the question and the
response in your notes.

Sixth, record your own insights, comments, and questions as they
occur to you during the lecture.

Seventh, develop your own catch phrases or codes that will save
you time. For example, if you want to remind yourself to compare
the issue being discussed in this class with one that was covered a

week before, you might want to write "c/c [compare and contrast] discussion on _____ [enter date]." Or use familiar symbols from other disciplines such as math, e.g., the = sign, or the ≠ sign (the equals sign with a line drawn through it to signify "not the same as"). Or before class, list in the margins all the key people or terms likely to be mentioned often in the day's class and assign abbreviations, such as their initials, to each of them. This way, in a lecture on Progressivism, you won't have to write Theodore Roosevelt a dozen times. Finally, be creative! Make up your own codes. One of the authors of this handbook made it through a class on the U.S. Constitution by writing "Csstus" for "Constitution" at least a million times in her notes!

If the class is a discussion class, steps 1 and 2 still apply. You will still want to jot down the main issues and points raised by your classmates, and you will still want to limit yourself to one or two examples that your classmates may provide in discussing each issue.

Finally, review, review, review. As soon as possible following a day's class, review your notes. Fill in missing verbs and punctuation so that, a month from now, the sentences make sense. Write a summary at the end of the day's notes, recapping the main themes and the most interesting points made. These mini-essays will be valuable when you study for the exam. Who knows? The professor may ask for a short essay on one of these very topics.

Why Are Class Discussions Important?

Some students let their minds drift off once the professor stops lecturing and the class discussion begins. But you're too smart to make that mistake. Class discussions help in at least four ways.

First, in the give and take of discussion, the main points of the day's topic are repeated and clarified.

Second, during the discussion, your classmates will provide analogies and examples that you will find useful.

Third, one of your classmates may raise a question that you are hesitant to raise but want answered.

Fourth, participating in a class discussion tests your ability to present your own views clearly and persuasively.

☞ *HELPING HAND* Learning to discuss a topic effectively with a diverse group of peers is a skill that will serve you well throughout your life. Remember: Don't monopolize the floor. Don't interrupt. Don't mumble. Most important, never try to make your point by insulting a classmate who disagrees with you. The same etiquette applies even more so to online postings where your words will not have the benefit of friendly body language and facial expressions. The Internet is replete with "flame-wars" that distract everyone from the topic at hand, so mastering the art of composing constructive criticism and fair dialogue is becoming as important in the world of instant online communication as it is in person.

Can I Ask the Professor for Help?

Some students think of the classroom as an adversarial situation—the professor against the students. Others think that the professor is too busy to be "bothered" by a visit or an email from a student. Still others think that a professor's office hours are only for students who fail an exam, want to drop out of a course, or have some life-threatening problem to relate that interferes with the course requirements. All these assumptions are wrong.

If you have a question about the assignments, the readings, or the topic of a class lecture or discussion, do talk to the professor. If you are having trouble organizing a paper for the class, ask for your professor's help. And if you did not do as well on an exam or a paper as you think you are capable of doing, ask your professor's advice on how to improve your work next time. You will not be imposing if you go during the professor's scheduled office hours. You can also ask, before or after class, if your professor would mind receiving an email from you.

Of course, there are limits. Don't ask a professor to explain a reading you haven't actually read. Don't expect a professor to reproduce a lecture or discussion class you missed. Don't ask for special treatment, such as getting the length of an assignment shortened or a deadline changed. Many professors offer an email address or a comment form on the course website for student questions outside of office hours. Remember, your professor may receive five, ten, even a hundred email messages from students each day. Although casual punctuation, familiar modes of address, incomplete sentences, and abbreviations are common in electronic communications among peers, treat an email to a professor much as you would a written letter. Address a professor as you would in class or in his or her office, provide a clear subject line so urgent items are easy to pick out of a sometimes very full inbox, explain in full sentences your question and comment, and sign the note with your full name and, if it has not come up in the body of the message, which of the professor's classes you are taking. Above all, remember that emails might not be read for several days depending on the professor's email routines, so bring all urgent matters up in person. And of course, be especially careful to be polite and respectful in your electronic postings as the emotions and motives of email messages are notoriously easy to misinterpret.

☞ *HELPING HAND*   If you have a problem or a question about the class or an assignment, discuss it with the professor immediately. Don't let it fester until after a test or after the assignment has been turned in. As those late-night advertisements on television always say: "Act now, before it's too late."

RECAP

This chapter provided a strategy for note taking, getting the most out of classroom discussions, and asking your professor for help. The key advice on note taking is to listen carefully for the major themes in the professor's lecture, don't bury yourself in details, and revise and review those class notes as soon as possible. The secret to getting the most out of classroom discussions is to listen, participate, and incorporate other people's ideas into your notes. Remember that the rule of thumb in seeking a professor's help is to ask for constructive advice not special treatment. And, finally, attending class and keeping up with your work are fundamental.

There's So Much Weekly Reading Assigned for the Class . . . How Can I Ever Do It All?

- *Why is this textbook so big?*
- *How can I make this textbook manageable?*
- *What do I highlight in the textbook?*

_T_IPS IN THIS CHAPTER

- ▪ Learning the function of a textbook
- ▪ Making the textbook manageable

Why Is This Textbook So Big?

In most courses, the textbook is a student's main study aid. It provides the basic narrative of the historical period you will be studying, and introduces you to the "who," "what," "when," and "why" for the semester's work. Generally, a textbook is bulky, imposing, and bursting with names, dates, and descriptions of events that may be unfamiliar to you. The result is that you may feel overwhelmed.

Why is the textbook so packed with information on so many topics? The authors of the textbook try to be as inclusive as possible, providing a broad portrait of the political, social, economic, military, diplomatic, and intellectual trends and developments of each historical era because they do not know which topics your professor—and the hundreds of other professors across the country—may choose to focus on for the semester. Because the textbook is inclusive rather than selective, your professors can be selective, confident that the textbook will fill in the gaps for each student.

How Can I Make the Textbook Manageable?

First, familiarize yourself with its format. Most textbooks will have a table of contents that previews the topics you are going to encounter in the book, a list of illustrations and special features that appear in the book, and an index at the end of the volume. Every textbook divides the historical material to be covered into manageable chapters, and each chapter is likely to have the following: an introduction, which lays out the major themes of the chapter; a time line and/or a chronological chart, which lists the main events covered in the chapter; the body of the chapter, divided into topical sections; illustrations, including maps, charts, graphs, photographs, or paintings relevant to the era; a summary, which recaps the main points of the chapter; a bibliography, which lists books or websites or films for further study of the period; and finally, one or two special features, such as a biography of a famous or typical person of the era.

Here is a sample table of contents of a chapter on the era following the Civil War, known as Reconstruction, in the textbook, *Making America*. See how many of the "clues" in the list that follows the outline you picked up as you read this table of contents.

Chapter 16 Reconstruction: High Hopes and Broken Dreams, 1865–1877
  Presidential Reconstruction
    Republican War Aims
    Lincoln's Approach to Reconstruction: "With Malice Toward None"
    Abolishing Slavery Forever: The Thirteenth Amendment
    Andrew Johnson and Reconstruction
    The Southern Response: Minimal Compliance
  Freedom and the Legacy of Slavery
    Defining the Meaning of Freedom
    Creating Communities
    Land and Labor
    The White South: Confronting Change
  Congressional Reconstruction
    Challenging Presidential Reconstruction
    The Civil Rights Act of 1866
    Defining Citizenship: The Fourteenth Amendment
    Radicals in Control: Impeachment of the President
    Political Terrorism and the Election of 1868
    Voting Rights and Civil Rights
  Individual Choices: Frederick Douglass
  Black Reconstruction
    The Republican Party in the South
    Creating an Educational System and Fighting Discrimination
    Railroad Development and Corruption
  The End of Reconstruction
    The "New Departure"
    The 1872 Election

```
     Redemption by Terror: The "Mississippi Plan"
     The Compromise of 1877
     After Reconstruction
  Summary
  Suggested Readings
```

How many of these clues did you pick up?

1. The title of the chapter provides the theme: much was expected but there were many failures during Reconstruction.
2. Reconstruction began in 1865 and ended in 1877—it will be important to know what events occurred in these twelve years [the end of the Civil War, 1865; the removal of federal troops from the South, 1877].
3. The table of contents is actually an outline of the Reconstruction era.
4. The textbook covers not only political developments of the era but also social and economic ones, as in the topics "Creating Communities" and "Land and Labor."
5. Key terms that you will want to write down and learn are listed here, such as "Mississippi Plan" and "the Civil Rights Act of 1866."
6. There were three different Reconstruction plans: presidential, congressional, and African American or black.
7. The special feature, "Individual Choices," suggests that individuals shape history by the choices they make.
8. The summary will provide a review of the key points from each of the sections of the chapter.
9. If you are doing a paper on Reconstruction, the "Suggested Readings" is a good place to start for a bibliography.

☞ *HELPING HAND*   Reading the table of contents for the chapter you are assigned makes good sense. The table of contents tells you what you can expect to find in the text; it introduces you to key terms and ideas. It only takes a few moments to read—time that is well spent!

What Do I Highlight in the Textbook?

Now that you know what to expect, you can move on to step two: resist the temptation to barge right in, armed with a highlighter or a pen, ready to underline every name, date, or event mentioned in the chapter.

Turning the whole chapter bright yellow or pink won't help much, even though it may make you feel like you are doing something! Instead, read the assigned chapter's introduction and summary *first*. They will tell you what is important to remember, consider—and highlight. Then, read the body of the chapter.

If, for example, the chapter introduction tells you that the focus will be on the events and policies during Reconstruction, you will want to highlight the names of key political figures during the era, such as President Johnson, and key legislation, such as the Fourteenth Amendment. In this particular textbook, *Making America,* the authors have gone a long way to assist you by including a running glossary on each page, in which key figures, key terms, and key events or legislation are defined for you. Other texts help you by printing these key terms in bold or italic type for you.

The same principle applies no matter what period of history you are studying. If the chapter introduction in a European textbook tells you that the focus will be on the causes of the French Revolution, you will want to highlight the names and descriptions of those acts or political decisions that heightened tensions between the government and the people, as well as any key information on economic problems, radical organizations, or ideological challenges to the monarchical system of government.

☞ *HELPING HAND*   Always review the summary of the chapter to see if you have taken special notice—by highlighting or note taking—of all the main points recapped for you by the author.

Now you are ready for the final step: testing yourself. For example, close the book and write your own short essay on the main themes of the chapter. Afterward, check the textbook introduction and summary to see if you left out anything important. Or list as many of the important people or events from the chapter as you can recall and then define and explain the significance of each item on your list. Save these self-tests. They will make excellent review materials for the professor's tests.

☞ *HELPING HAND*   Never skip words or terms in the text that you don't understand. You know what you should do: look them up!

Many textbooks have companion websites or electronic versions of the book itself. Take full advantage of the quizzes, interactive exercises, videos, maps, and primary sources contained on those websites. Many of these exercises are automatically corrected and can give you instant feedback on what areas you might have missed in your first reading of the chapter. Take special note of primary sources and maps that amplify, complicate, or extend the arguments of the textbook. Your professor will be thrilled when you bring those items up in class discussion as it will mean you are not just learning history as it was written in the textbook but also practicing the art of historical detection.

RECAP

This chapter showed you how to make the textbook a tool for learning, not just a heavy load in your backpack.

How Do I Study for History Tests?

- *What kinds of tests will I take in class?*
- *How can I improve my performance on these in-class tests?*
- *How do I complete the take-home essay exam?*
- *How do I complete online tests?*
- *How do I study for any test?*

What Kinds of Tests Will I Take in Class?

No matter what you call it—test, exam, quiz, evaluation—that moment of truth is bound to strike a little terror in the heart of any student. Perhaps it will help if you know what types of tests you are likely to encounter in a college history class.

1. The *quiz* **and its many variations:**
   a. **The map quiz.**   The professor asks you to fill in certain key items, such as national boundaries, important rivers, capital cities, mountain ranges, disputed territories, or the nations forming various political alliances.
   b. **The pop quiz on a specific reading.**   For this surprise test (one that is "popped" on you without warning) the professor requires that you answer a set of questions on the reading assigned for that day or week.
   c. **The pop quiz on basic information.**   Again, without prior warning, the professor examines you on fundamental facts, such as critical dates, names of treaties or wars, or historical events, to discover if you have mastered the basic information needed to move on to an analysis of the material.

2. **Identification:** The professor asks you to identify, define, and usually give the significance of a term, person, event, piece of legislation, treaty, etc.

3. **Time line or chronology:** The professor asks you to place a series of events in chronological order.

4. **The multiple-choice exam:** For each question, a number of possible answers are provided. You are expected to select the answer that is correct from among these choices. For example,

The Declaration of Sentiments of 1848 was modeled after what earlier landmark document in American history?
   A. The Constitution
   B. The Articles of Confederation
   C. The Virginia and Kentucky Resolves
   D. The Declaration of Independence

Another example would be:

The Magna Carta clarified the relationship between
   A. English wives and husbands.
   B. The king and the barons.
   C. The House of Commons and the House of Lords.
   D. English merchants and farmers.

By the way, the answer to question 1 is "D"; the answer to question 2 is "B."

5. **The in-class essay exam:** The professor requires you to write one or more essays, each with a thesis statement that is developed through examples and that has a conclusion. The question may require you, for example, to take a pro or con side in an historical debate, to compare and contrast two movements or historical events, or to explain the causes and consequences of a major historical decision. This exam can be an **open-book exam,** a test in which you are allowed to consult your texts and your own notes, or it may be a **closed-book exam,** a test in which you cannot consult any of these resources.

How Can I Improve My Performance on These In-Class Tests?

For any in-class exam or quiz, the important thing is: don't panic! Take a deep breath. Then, follow these tips:

1. Before you pick up your pen or turn on your computer, read the instructions carefully so that you understand what the professor wants you to do and how he or she wants it done.

2. Take a moment to read all the questions carefully.
3. Now prioritize your time. Are there questions you can answer easily? Answer them first. Are there questions you know you can answer but you will need to dig deep for the necessary information? Answer them next. Leave the questions that stump you for the end.
4. Be sure to leave yourself enough time to reread and, if necessary, revise your answers. Make sure you answered the specific question you were asked.
5. Finally, whatever you write, make it legible as well as intelligible. Tiny, cramped handwriting; messy pages filled with crossed-out material and arrows pointing everywhere; and lots of curly-ques on those g's or y's are likely to alienate the professor. She's only human, after all.

How Do I Complete the Take-Home Essay Exam?

The questions are similar to those in the in-class essay exam, but the professor may set higher standards for grammar, punctuation, organization, and number of examples cited or details provided, and he may expect a longer essay because you will have more time than you have in the in-class exam. He may also require footnotes to any sources you consult because you write the essays at home.

How Do I Complete Online Tests?

Many professors now use the computer for exams and quizzes. Although you should use the same study strategies for these tests, the format will be different from in-class exams. On the day of the test, a link on the course website will appear or the professor will give you the URL in class with instructions on how to take the test. Make sure you are aware of any time limits the professor might set. Must the test be taken during certain hours? Will the website you're using automatically shut down when the time allotted for the test runs out? Can you go back and change something once you've hit the "Submit" or "OK" button?

For multiple-choice tests, you will probably be given a list of questions, each followed by several possible answers. Every answer will have a box next to it. When you find the right answer, click the mouse on the correct box. At the bottom of the webpage will be different kinds of hyperlinks. Some might tell you to continue to the next page, while

others might say "Submit" or "OK." Usually when you hit "Submit" or "OK," you are submitting the exam to the professor and will not be able to change any answers.

For map quizzes, there will be some kind of mechanism such as drag and drop for placing a name or number on the map.

For essay exams, the most common format acts much like a bulletin board. The form will have questions and then large boxes underneath them for you to type in your answer. You can either type your answers directly on the form or you can write the text on a word-processing program and then copy and paste the material into the form. For anything longer than a sentence, strongly consider writing your essay in a word processor, saving frequently, using spell check, and proofreading carefully because websites can behave unpredictably. Many a precious student response has been lost when the browser accidentally closed or a new webpage unexpectedly loaded into the same browser window. To send the exam to the professor, hit the "Submit" or "OK" button at the bottom of the screen.

Some course websites allow tests to be taken in a practice or study mode. Take advantage of such opportunities to iron out any technical glitches you might have otherwise encountered on the official test, to calm your nerves before the real thing, and to uncover gaps in your preparation. Pay special attention to the feedback, if any, provided on incorrect answers as these messages often include hints about the correct answer and even direct references or links to the relevant areas of the textbook.

☞ *HELPING HAND*   Always look over your answers before submitting the exam to the professor. And make sure you answered the question that the professor asked.

How Do I Study for Any Test?

Remember the Boy Scout motto: be prepared. It's the best advice, not only for those wilderness survival trips but also for taking a history exam.

1. **Keep current in your assignments.** This is crucial for handling pop quizzes, but it also applies to exams that are scheduled.

2. **Review your class notes regularly.** Instead of that frantic effort to memorize material the night before the exam, reading and reviewing your notes calmly each week may yield surprising results: you will actually remember more than you ever thought possible.

3. **Review the chapter introductions and summaries in your main texts before the exam.** Remember: these chapter sections contain the essentials.

4. **Familiarize yourself with typical formats for essay questions.** Professors who want analysis and evaluation rather than description are likely to ask questions in these formats:

   a. *Compare and contrast.* For example, compare and contrast the way in which French colonizers and English colonizers interacted with the Native Americans in the seventeenth and eighteenth centuries. Or compare and contrast the political platforms of the Populist party and the Republican party in the election of 1896.

   b. *Evaluate the pros and cons of the following statement.* For example, evaluate the claim by some historians that dropping the atomic bomb on Japan was a justifiable military strategy during World War II. Or evaluate the pros and cons of the following statement: Slavery caused the Civil War.

c. *What are the causes and/or consequences of . . . .* For example, what are the main causes for the failure of the Revolution of 1848? Or what were the causes and the consequences of the 1896 Supreme Court decision in *Plessy v. Ferguson?*

5. **Review old quizzes or exams to gauge your strengths and weaknesses.** Did the professor comment on the same problems in each of your earlier exams? For example, was your organization poor in several instances? Do you notice that you often lost credit for answers that were not specific enough or did not contain enough examples? Did you consistently run out of time when writing an in-class exam? Or did the professor consistently praise your writing style or organization of the essay? Now that you know your strengths and weaknesses, it's time to develop a strategy for emphasizing the former and improving the latter. Poor organization? Try outlining your answer before you begin to write. You ran out of time? Answer the questions you find easiest first. You didn't provide enough examples? Get into the habit of listing two examples for every major point you are making. Check to make sure you have included both when you read over your answer.

☞ *HELPING HAND*   Until it becomes an automatic process, you might have to say in your essay, "Two examples that come to mind," or "To illustrate the point, I will offer two examples." This is perfectly acceptable.

6. **Review available websites for the textbook or the course for sample or practice quizzes that might allow you to test your memory of key people, places, and ideas; primary sources that might make telling examples in an essay exam; and supplemental materials such as lecture notes and presentations the professor posted as the term progressed.**

7. **Create your own practice multiple-choice questions, your own short answers, and even your own essay questions, using the textbook, assigned readings, and your class notes.**

8. **Find a study partner.** Have him write a dozen multiple-choice questions for you; write a dozen for him. Discuss possible exam topics— and possible answers. Remember: two heads can sometimes be better than one.

9. **Create other tools, such as time lines or chronologies, to help you master the material being tested.**

☞ *HELPING HAND*   Remember that some students excel when they are given an in-class exam—their adrenaline starts flowing and off they go. Others do best on take-home exams—they like to ponder, outline their thoughts, revise, and polish. Some students get a sinking feeling in the pit of their stomach when they take tests, but they really enjoy writing research papers or book critiques. Very few of us do everything well. Get to know your own preferences—learn what comes naturally and what is a struggle. Then—you guessed it—put some extra time and work into improving in the areas that aren't easy for you.

RECAP

This chapter helped ease your fears about tests. It described the various types of tests you will encounter, from simple quizzes to take-home essay exams to online tests. Then it took you step by step through the best way to prepare for these tests—and do well on them. The keys to success are to keep up with the class assignments, review your notes, and learn from your past mistakes.

How Can Maps Help Me Understand History?

- *What are the different kinds of maps?*
- *How do I read a map?*
- *How can I test my map-reading skills?*

You stuff maps in your glove compartment in case you get lost on your next trip. You check the station stops on a rumbling subway car when you travel underground in New York, San Francisco, Boston, or Washington, D.C. You follow your plane's flight path on the map you find in the airline's complimentary magazine. Trail maps guide you along the hiking path; pirate's treasure maps appear in the old movies you remember watching; and when you turn on your television, you can watch your local meteorologist draw clouds, raindrops, and smiley-faced suns on a weather map. In short, maps are a useful part of your daily life. Can they be useful in your college history class? The answer, of course, is yes.

The maps you find in your college history textbook are not there to help you find the best route from Houston, Texas, to Salt Lake City, Utah. They won't tell you whether to bring a raincoat to class. If you read maps correctly, however, they will help you understand historical events and developments by reinforcing visually what has been described in the text. Maps provide you with a different way of conceptualizing, a different way of taking in information. To use them well, however, you must know how to read them.

What Are the Different Kinds of Maps?

Cartographers, or mapmakers, produce several different types of maps. The most common types are described in the following paragraphs.

Physical Maps

Physical maps provide visual representations of the physical features of an area of the world, including oceans, continents, rivers, and mountains. Often the elevations of a mountain range or the depths of a valley are shown by a particular color chosen by the mapmaker to reinforce the differences in the topography, or physical features of the earth. Historians find these maps useful in illustrating a relationship between people and the natural world that they have introduced in the text. For example, you can read that Hannibal's crossing the Alps was a miraculous feat, but you may not grasp just how impressive it was until you look at a map illustrating the obstacles presented to a third-century B.C. army by this towering mountain range. Or you can read that seventeenth-century Chesapeake planters settled along riverbanks, but you may not fully appreciate the wisdom of their choices until you see a map of Virginia and Maryland's waterways and their connection to the Atlantic Ocean. You can hear a professor discuss how European explorers of the fifteenth century changed shipping patterns in the Indian Ocean, but a map showing currents and winds would more graphically illustrate how weather dictated the schedules of the earlier sailors but did not have such a hold over the Europeans, with their new technologies.

☞ *HELPING HAND*   You can use physical maps as a window into the technological and scientific limitations and advances of an historical era. After the voyages of Christopher Columbus and other European explorers, sixteenth-century cartographers attempted to re-map the globe. Without aerial photography, sophisticated computer-based measurement techniques, or other modern technological aids, they were limited to drawing maps based on first-hand and sometimes second-hand descriptions by ship captains, soldiers, and sailors. Comparing those maps with modern maps may help you appreciate the impact of modern technology on our perceptions of the world.

Political Maps

Political maps show how political decision making shapes the world in which we live. They show national, state, province, or county boundaries and the location of cities and towns within the borders of a nation. Traditionally, boundaries between countries are drawn in thick, black lines and countries are given distinctive colors. You have been using these maps since elementary school, when teachers asked you to fill in the names of the states or to mark the location of state capitals. Historians use them to provide critical visual information. For example, the location of Belgium is a key element in any discussion of German military strategy and French and English responses to it in World War I. Using a series of maps that show the changing national borders on the continent of Africa from 1900 to 2000 will open the door to understanding European colonialism and African independence movements. For a striking comparison, a history text might place a distribution map showing languages and religions next to a map showing the borders of African states created during the era of European colonization. Looking at these maps, you can begin to explore the problems that were created for the African peoples living in each of these artificially created states or nations.

> ☞ *HELPING HAND*   Remember that you can read political maps as just that: political. They reveal power relationships among nations, social classes, races, or political parties within a nation. The right to establish national boundaries, like the right to establish the boundaries of a voting district or to decide where a national capital will be located, provides valuable clues to who wields authority and power in an historical era.

Transportation Maps

Transportation maps show land, sea, or air routes. Imagine trying to follow European exploration of the Americas without a map showing Columbus's sea route or Magellan's voyage around the world. Or consider the advantages of seeing, on a map, the difficult overland route followed by American settlers along the Oregon Trail. Transportation maps can also help you see how the movement of people is linked to the movement of ideas and even disease. For example, a map showing the trade routes from the Mediterranean to India after the eighth century can provide important clues to the rapid spread of Islam across the Asian continent. A map showing that European trading patterns before 1492 did not cross the Atlantic Ocean will help you understand the dramatic impact of contact between the New World and the Old—a contact that brought new and often deadly diseases into the lives of both the Amerindians and the Europeans.

Distribution Maps

Distribution maps focus on the occurrence of one or two special features, for example, rainfall in various regions, population density in a nation's cities, or agricultural specialization within a state. A map showing the distribution of Democratic, Liberty Party, and Republican votes in the presidential election of 1860 is certain to help a student of the Civil War understand the impact of sectionalism and the breakdown of national party systems. Similarly, a map showing the population of major European cities before and after the Black Plague will bring home the impact of disease on the history of Late Medieval Europe. Finally, a map showing the distribution of various diseases in Africa will help you understand why it took so long for Europe to colonize that continent.

☞ *HELPING HAND*   Don't forget that many maps are a combination
of types. A mapmaker assigned to illustrate the journeys of Marco
Polo might include the national boundaries that this Italian adven-
turer crossed, the physical features he confronted along the way,
and the land routes that he followed.

Interactive Maps

Many history textbooks and courses now incorporate maps in digital
form. At their best, these maps allow many different layers of information to be shown in exciting new combinations and controls that allow
you to turn on and off different types of information. An interactive
map of the trans-Atlantic slave trade, for example, might animate the
magnitude and destinations of successive waves of slave importation,
overlaid perhaps with informational layers about prevailing winds,
currents, even pirate activity. Such maps are powerful learning and research tools. When you encounter one, be sure to explore it fully and
consider the relationship between all the historical factors on display.
Internet-based mapping projects such as Google Earth provide spectac-
ularly detailed images of terrain, settlement patterns, and nearby points
of interest for almost any historical location in your textbook. With such
products, you can "fly" up to Peruvian silver mines from the sixteenth
century, follow the trail of Lewis and Clark over the mountains, or sail
along the New England coast in search of the Northwest Passage.

How Do I Read a Map?

Most maps have several standard features that you will need to
understand.

First, the *scale* tells you the relationship between the size of an area
on a map and the size of that same area on the earth. The scale can be indicated in various ways, but most maps in a history book have a bar or
line in one corner of the map that is divided into sections that represent
actual distance. One inch on that bar, for example, can equal 25 miles.

Second, *direction* is shown on the map by a grid of parallels and
meridians. Many maps also have a *compass rose* that shows you north,
south, east, and west. Although a map can be oriented in any direction,
traditionally north is at the top.

Third, the *legend* provides a key to the symbols for all the features
you will encounter on the map. For example, cities are usually indicated
by dots; the larger the dot, the bigger the city. International boundaries,
state or provincial boundaries, and county boundaries are indicated by

broken lines of different shape or thickness. A star is often the symbol for the capital of a nation or a state.

Finally, the *title* of a historical map alerts you to the type of information that the mapmaker is illustrating.

How Can I Test My Map-Reading Skills?

Are you ready to test your map-reading skills? Below are three maps.

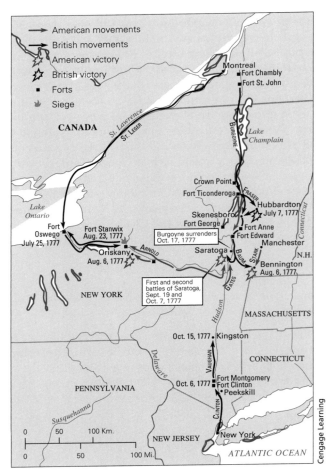

MAP 4.1 The Burgoyne Campaign, 1777 *The defeat of General John Burgoyne and his army at Saratoga was a major turning point in the war. This map shows American and British troop movement and the locations and dates of the Saratoga battles leading to the British surrender.*

The first map is entitled "The Burgoyne Campaign, 1777," and it illustrates one of the most important turning points in the American Revolution—the defeat of a major British army by the Americans. What is the scale of this map? What physical features are indicated on the map? What special features are indicated in the legend? What type of map would you say best describes this first example?

The second map is entitled "Presidential Election, 1828." Why did the mapmaker feel that a scale and a compass rose were unnecessary? What information is provided in the legend? Who won the election? How does the map make this point clearer to you?

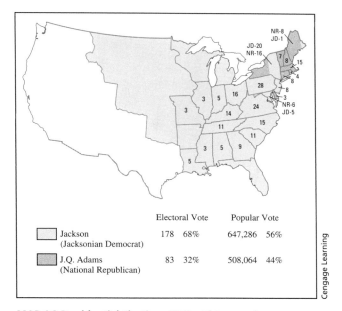

MAP 4.2 Presidential Election, 1828   *This map shows how the political coalition between Andrew Jackson and Martin Van Buren turned the tables in the election of 1828. Jackson's Democratic Party won every region except Adams's native New England.*

The third map is entitled "The African Slave Trade, 1500–1800." In what sense could you call this a transportation map? How does the map-maker indicate where the majority of slaves came from and where the majority were taken? Were all the slaves transported to the Americas?

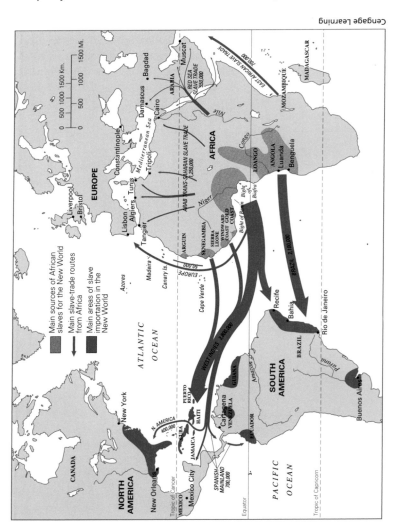

Map 4.3 The African Slave Trade, 1500–1800 *After 1500, a vast new trade in slaves from sub-Saharan Africa to the Americas joined the ongoing slave trade to the Islamic states of North Africa, the Middle East, and India. The West Indies were the major destination of the Atlantic slave trade, followed by Brazil.*

☞ *HELPING HAND* Remember that historians and history professors use maps to illustrate important points about events, developments, and human decision making in the past. Your professor will probably want you to consider the implications of the information provided on the map rather than memorize that information.

RECAP

This chapter introduced you to maps as historical tools; it described the different types of maps you are likely to encounter and it explained the common elements you will find on a map. It also provided you with some examples that allow you to test your map-reading skills.

5

H ow Can I Work Effectively with Primary, Secondary, and Fictional Sources in My History Class?

- *What is a primary source?*
- *What is a secondary source?*
- *What questions should I ask when I analyze or evaluate sources?*
- *What does the professor mean when he or she asks for the historical context of a document?*
- *Why do my sources disagree?*
- *Why did my professor assign a piece of fiction in a history class— and how do I evaluate it?*

In addition to the textbook, most professors will assign a list of specialized readings, films, or illustrative materials. The professor will often want you to do more than simply read or view these assignments; she will want you to analyze or evaluate them. To do this, you will need to ask—and answer—a few basic questions about each of them.

What Is a Primary Source?

To the historian, *primary sources* are the basic "stuff" of history. A *primary source* is any document or artifact from the period under study. It was written or created by a person who lived through the events being described. Primary sources include, but are not limited to: diaries, journals, and correspondence; government records or documents; public speeches; newspapers, pamphlets, broadsides, or books; portraits, landscape paintings, maps, photographs or films; and the records of military, religious, business, or charitable institutions. Although many primary sources have been published in collections of documents, most are held by historical societies or archives, university and public libraries, or government offices. When historians do research, they usually have to go to one of these archives to read the primary sources they need for their project. In the past few decades, happily, millions of primary sources have been digitized by the nation's leading libraries, putting thousands of complete collections of documents within reach of anyone with a computer keyboard. Be careful, however, to remember that most of these sources are not visible to search engines such as Google; they can only be found by visiting the websites of libraries such as the Library of Congress and entering your search terms into their private catalog. In some fields, the best archives are restricted to subscribers and must be accessed through your campus library or with your university computer credentials. Nonetheless, undergraduates have an unprecedented opportunity to do authentic primary source research.

You are probably already familiar with several famous primary sources, such as the Magna Carta, the Declaration of Independence, the Communist Manifesto, or Hammurabi's Code. In high school you may have read one of these well-known diaries or autobiographies: the autobiography of Benjamin Franklin, the journals of Marco Polo, or Anne Frank's diary. But primary sources do not have to be the work of famous figures; the correspondence between an ordinary Civil War soldier and his wife, the photo albums your grandmother creates, and the tax records your parents store in their filing cabinet are also primary sources.

Here's an excerpt from a primary source you are likely to recognize immediately.

We the people of the United States, in order to form a more perfect union, establish justice, insure domestic tranquility, provide for the common defense, promote the general welfare, and secure the blessings of liberty to ourselves and our posterity, do ordain and establish this Constitution for the United States of America.

If you said that it is the preamble to the U.S. Constitution, you are right. Here's another excerpt that you won't recognize, yet it fits the criteria for a primary source. This is a statement by a Pennsylvania delegate on the floor of the Constitutional Convention of 1787, recorded in the minutes of the convention and also in James Madison's own secret journal of the debates at that convention.

Life and liberty were generally said to be of more value than property. An accurate view of the matter would, nevertheless, prove that property was the main object of society. . . .

Finally, here is an excerpt from a letter by New York lawyer, and later Chief Justice of the first Supreme Court, John Jay, to George Washington, who would become the first president of the United States if the new Constitution was ratified, or approved, by nine states. Jay was a delegate to New York's ratifying convention.

There is much Reason to believe that the Majority of the Convention of this State will be composed of anti foederal [the antifederalists opposed the Constitution] Characters: but it is doubtful whether the Leaders will be able to govern the Party. Many in the opposition are Friends to the Union and mean well, but their principle Leaders are very far from being solicitous about the Fate of the Union.

Not all primary sources are written sources. Here is a portrait of Thomas Jefferson, the third president of the United States, showing Jefferson's preference for plain, informal clothing rather than the elegant dress of European aristocrats.

© Bettmann/CORBIS COLLECTION

This early nineteenth-century engraving by Thomas Sully captures the former president in his customary greatcoat, unadorned suit, and well-worn boots. Thomas Jefferson (1743–1826), third U.S. president. Engraving after illustration by Thomas Sully (last portrait from life).

Public documents, records of a political meeting, a private letter to a friend, paintings of Thomas Jefferson's inauguration—each of these primary sources hold clues to the motives, attitudes, and political philosophies of the people of the era. For a good historian, they are all critical pieces of the puzzle of the past.

☞ *HELPING HAND* Don't make the mistake of believing that all primary sources are old, written on faded and yellowing paper, or written with a quaint vocabulary. The first test you take in a history class on the Constitution could be a primary source document for someone, five years from now, writing a paper on students' views on the Constitutional Convention! In fact, you are creating primary sources every day: photos taken on a summer vacation, college admissions essays, tax returns, letters home to your parents asking for money, and your first college transcript.

What Is a Secondary Source?

A *secondary source* is any document or artifact that was created after the period under study has passed. It is usually an assessment or analysis of, or commentary on, events or people of the past. Secondary sources include, but are not limited to: scholarly monographs or books, scholarly articles in journals, biographies, and historical novels or films.

Again, you have probably read many secondary sources during your school career. If your high school history teacher assigned a book on the coming of the American Revolution such as Edmund Morgan's *The Stamp Act Crisis* or you did a book report on Eric Foner's biography *Tom Paine,* then you have already worked with secondary sources. Perhaps you read a biography of Queen Elizabeth, a novel about the Civil War, or an article in *American Heritage Magazine* about the battle of the Alamo. Even the textbook for this college history course qualifies as a secondary source.

Here are the concluding paragraphs of a book written in 1986 by Christopher Collier and James Lincoln Collier, entitled *Decision at Philadelphia: The Constitutional Convention of 1787.* Notice that it assesses the delegates to the convention and their achievements. The authors speak as analysts, not as participants, in the events of 1787.

The writers of the American Constitution were not angels. They made mistakes: they left out a bill of rights, they did not confront the question of judicial review, and most tragically, they were

so much people of their time that they could not
see that blacks were as human as they were. But
withal, they rose above themselves far more than
most men would have done in their place. And the
generations of Americans who have grown up under
the Constitution they struggled so hard to make
are eternally in their debt.

☞ *HELPING HAND*   Sometimes a source can be either primary or
secondary. It all depends on how it is being used. An historian
analyzing changing attitudes of other historians toward the men
who wrote the Constitution would see the Colliers' book as a
primary source.

What Questions Should I Ask When I Analyze or Evaluate Sources?

Reading a primary or a secondary source intelligently requires that
you be a good detective. Like Sherlock Holmes, you need to search
for clues.

Some questions you might want to ask about primary sources
are obvious: Who wrote it, and why? Who is the audience for this
source? If it is a public document, was it a campaign speech, a policy
statement, a judicial ruling? Is it a private letter? If so, is it written to
a loved one, a friend, or an enemy? Is it a diary entry, intended only
for the diary-keeper to read? Is the document propaganda? Is it po-
lemical? Is it didactic; that is, is the author's intention to instruct or
educate? Where did the document appear in print? In a newspaper?
In a prestigious journal or a glossy magazine? In a religious publication? In a pamphlet issued by a nonprofit organization or a special
interest group?

If it is a secondary source, you might want to learn the credentials
of the author. Does the author have an obvious political or ideological
bias—or a hidden one? Is the book or article intended for a general
audience or is it a scholarly work? And, most important of all perhaps,
what claims does the author make, what interpretation does he offer,
and what evidence does he provide to back up his argument?

What Does the Professor Mean When He or She Asks for the Historical Context of a Document?

The historical context is, simply, the circumstances in which the document was generated. What was happening at the time, in the author's personal life or in the world around her, that might have prompted the document to be written or might have shaped how it was written and what was said? What was the intellectual climate of the time? That is, what were the accepted "truths" about human nature, the roles of men and women, and other fundamental issues? Did people explain events in religious terms? In scientific terms? Was the author's society prosperous or poor? Did the author live in times of crisis and war or in peace?

For example, what was the historical context for the Declaration of Independence? We know that the relationship between Great Britain and the colonies was in crisis in 1776. Over a decade of political debate and public demonstrations had occurred as colonists protested British policies and articulated their views on the proper role of government. We know also that the author of the Declaration of Independence, Thomas Jefferson, represented an elite group of educated and wealthy colonists who were widely read in Enlightenment philosophy, seventeenth-century English liberal thought, and the history of ancient republics. These elements of the historical context provide powerful clues to why the Declaration of Independence was issued, what arguments it chose to make, and why it persuaded many colonists to join the Revolution.

What was the historical context for the work of historian Eric Foner, whose prize-winning study, *Reconstruction,* argued persuasively that African Americans played important roles in shaping government policy during and after the Civil War and in creating new social institutions for freedmen and -women? Important clues lie in the fact that Foner's generation, many of them political activists in the civil rights movement in the late 1950s and 1960s, produced a school of historians known as "revisionists." One of the central goals of the revisionists was to rewrite U.S. history so that minorities, or "marginalized" peoples such as African Americans, Indians, women, and workers, were seen as active agents in shaping their destinies rather than as passive recipients.

Remember, understanding the historical context of a document is only the beginning of your analysis, not an end in itself. Don't ignore the content just because you have placed it and the author in their historical place and time.

☞ *HELPING HAND*   Think of yourself as a detective, ferreting out clues about the author of the document and the moment in history in which that author wrote. Every clue to the past has a history of its own!

Why Do My Sources Disagree?

Every student who has ever watched a police drama knows that people who witness the same event often have different accounts of it. The thief was tall; the thief was short; his coat was blue; his coat was gray. The first-hand accounts, or primary sources, you may deal with in a history class may disagree with one another just as dramatically. This is also true with secondary sources, because the historian's job is not only to re-create events of the past but to interpret and analyze them. Two excellent scholars may well come to different conclusions. Consider the excerpts below from two respected historians of the Nazi movement, Christopher R. Browning and Daniel Jonah Goldhagen. Both scholars seek to explain why ordinary men and women supported Hitler and, in particular, why these ordinary people were capable of acts of atrocity.

Browning examines the actions of a reserve police battalion who participated in the massacre of Jews at Jozefow. He concludes:

. . . [T]he collective behavior of Reserve Police Battalion 101 has deeply disturbing implications. There are many societies afflicted by traditions of racism and caught in the siege mentality of war or threat of war. Everywhere society conditions people to respect and defer to authority, and indeed could scarcely function otherwise. Everywhere people seek career advancement. In every modern society, the complexity of life and the resulting bureaucratization and specialization attenuate the sense of personal responsibilities of those implementing official policy. Within virtually every social collective, the peer group exerts tremendous pressures on behavior and sets moral norms.

```
If the men of Reserve Police Battalion 101 could
become killers under such circumstances, what group
of men cannot?
```

Goldhagen disagrees. He believes that a unique set of values and attitudes shared by the German people led to Nazism and the Holocaust, or mass murder of Jewish citizens. He writes:

```
The beliefs that were already the common property
of the German people upon Hitler's assumption of
power and which led the German people to assent
and contribute to the eliminationist measures of
the 1930's [the concentration camps, for example]
were the beliefs that prepared not just the Germans
who by circumstances, chance or choice ended up as
perpetrators but also the vast majority of the German
people to understand, assent to, and, when possible,
do their part to further the extermination, root
and branch, of the Jewish people. German political
culture had evolved to the point where an enormous
number of ordinary, representative Germans became—
and most of the rest of their fellow Germans were
fit to be—Hitler's willing executioners.
```

Both scholars examine the evidence, yet they come to dramatically different conclusions. If you look closely, you will see that, behind their conclusions, are a set of assumptions about human behavior. Browning assumes that all societies require certain attitudes—respect for authority and obedience to those in command—to function properly and that, under certain stressful conditions, people of any nation would have behaved as the German people behaved. Goldhagen argues that societies develop quite different sets of values and attitudes and that, over time, they develop distinctive cultures. He feels that there were elements in the German culture that made the German citizens accept and even embrace the racism of Nazism.

Was Germany unique or typical? Scholars have been asking this question for decades and coming up with different answers. You may not come up with the final answer, but you can subject the work of these two scholars to some of the useful questions covered above. What is the historical context for the two works? Did one write immediately after the war and one many decades later? Did either of these men fight in the war? Is one of them part of a revisionist movement in his field? Many of the questions raised in the section of this handbook that discussed how to evaluate your sources might help as well.

Why Did My Professor Assign a Piece of Fiction in a History Class—and How Do I Evaluate It?

You may ask yourself, What's a novel doing in a class assignment on the Industrial Revolution? Or perhaps you ask yourself, Why am I being asked to read a collection of poems when the topic on the syllabus is the Civil War? History professors often assign fiction or poetry related to the era under discussion because novelists or poets can provide rich, compelling descriptions of an era and its people. The characters created by a novelist or a poet can dramatize and personalize many of the changes, crises, or problems faced by the real people of an era. For example, you might understand the impact of European ideas and values on African society by reading *Things Fall Apart*, Chinua Achebe's richly detailed story of life in a traditional Nigerian village before and after the arrival of Christian missionaries. Or you and your classmates might understand more fully the rise of chivalry and its rituals in medieval Europe by reading *The Song of Roland*.

RECAP

This chapter introduced you to the two types of sources you and all other historians use while conducting research—primary sources and secondary sources—and it walked you through the questions you need to ask as you evaluate those sources, especially questions about the historical context in which the document was produced. Finally, it explained what that novel was doing on a history reading list and why it can be an important source for understanding the past.

CHAPTER 6

*H*ow Do I Manage Written Assignments?

■ *What sample assignments might I find in my history class?*

TIPS IN THIS CHAPTER

- Keeping a journal
- Writing a book review
- Writing a critical essay
- Participating in bulletin board discussions

Like most people, professors know the value of variety. During the course of the semester, your professor may ask you to grapple with other kinds of assignments besides papers, presentations, and exams. Her goal is not to throw you off guard; she is simply trying to bring history to life by allowing you to act the part of different historical characters or debate different political positions.

☞ *HELPING HAND*   For any of the assignments listed below, consider showing your professor a rough draft of your work a few days before the due date. This gives you time to get, and make use of, valuable assistance that will probably translate into a better final grade. Remember: the professor cannot help you if you do not ask for help.

What Sample Assignments Might I Find in My History Class?

Journals

Professors assign weekly or monthly journals to illustrate more vividly the importance of journal writing for the study of history. In the computer and telephone age, people rarely write diaries or journals. For centuries, however, this was a common means by which people organized their thoughts and described their lives.

Journals written by historical figures such as Abigail Adams, Marco Polo, or Christopher Columbus will appear in class syllabi. Reading them provides you with an invaluable insight into their thoughts and their activities at pivotal moments in world history. But writing your own journal will give you added insight into the experiences and motivations of these men and women. You will discover that it is more difficult to articulate your opinions on paper than in your own mind. As you write your own journal, going through the same process as these other journal writers, you will be better equipped to analyze their words and deeds. You will recognize, for example, how opinions change as external circumstances change. Did Marco Polo's views of non-Europeans change during the course of his travels? If so, why did they change? What were the circumstances surrounding his change of opinion?

The first step in journal writing is to do the assignment required by the professor. Even if she collects the journals only once or twice during the semester, you have to keep up with the work. If the professor requires you to write in your journal once a week, write in it once a week. Don't wait until the deadline to write out three or four quick entries. The professor wants to see the progression of your views, which may change dramatically as new information comes to light in the classroom and the class readings.

The second step is to think of the journal in the same way you think of any other written assignment. In other words, you should follow all grammar and spelling rules. Finally, make sure you follow the professor's instructions. Some journal assignments require that you give personal insights about your own life; some ask you to analyze the different readings and topics in class. If you do not understand the assignment, ask the professor to clarify what he wants.

Book Reviews

Book reviews are not the same as book reports. Book reviews analyze the main themes of a book rather than simply providing summaries of the plot. Avoid the book report pitfall by remembering that the professor has read the book and doesn't need you to describe what happened in it. He has given you this assignment because he wants to know if you are capable of picking out the most important aspects of the story and analyzing them. A book review of *The Diary of Anne Frank* should *not* look like this:

```
Anne, her family, and a few of their friends had to
hide in an attic because the Nazis were trying to
arrest and deport all the Jews living in Amsterdam.
In the attic, they had to remain quiet all day so
no-one would detect them. At night, they had quiet
conversations and Anne wrote in her diary. Friends
brought them food and the news every day.
```

Read the Book   You will not be able to write a credible book review unless you read the book. Crib notes and the film version (if available) are *never* a substitute for actually reading the book yourself.

While reading, take notes about the major plot points, and the themes and views expressed by each of the characters, making sure to write down the pertinent page numbers. If you do not take organized notes, you will have a much harder time trying to put together an analysis later. You do not want to waste time flipping through the pages trying to find that quote that you "distinctly" remember was somewhere in the middle of the book.

When you have finished reading the book, write down a short, one- or two-paragraph summary of the plot. This brief summary should help draw out the main themes, not just serve as a chronological list of events.

Now you are ready to write an outline or list of the major themes that will help you identify the thesis of the book review. For *The Diary of Anne Frank*, three possible themes might be:

1. Nazi persecution of the Jews throughout Europe
2. Psychological and material survival techniques used by the inhabitants of the attic
3. Anne's own problems with adolescence, compounded by the problems presented by living in an attic

The list above highlights Anne's particular problems, but it also addresses the larger question of how people coped with the Holocaust. Your thesis, then, might be the importance of case studies in analyzing larger historical phenomena.

Before you begin to develop your thesis further, you should do some research on Anne Frank herself. Knowing who the author is and why she wrote the book will provide insight into the themes the author raises and his or her perspective. Anne Frank actually lived through the events of the Holocaust, so her insights are probably very different from those of an author in the United States who had friends or relatives fighting in World War II but did not experience the war or persecution first-hand. Be sure to include any relevant information about the author in your review.

You might decide you need to do additional research for your review. Anne Frank's diary, for example, includes very little about the policies of the Nazis during World War II that led to her life in the attic. To place Anne's story within the historical context of World War II, you will need to read some secondary sources on this subject.

The next step is to write a thesis paragraph that sets out the main argument of your review. The thesis should make use of the themes you identified in your outline. You will probably need to provide a brief summary of the book, stressing the points that relate to your thesis. Don't just fill in paper space with details! End the review with a concluding paragraph that restates the thesis and the main themes that support it.

Critical Essays

It has finally happened: your instructor has given you your first big writing assignment: an essay analyzing an important historical figure, event, or topic. Is that panic or anticipation you feel in the pit of your stomach? Don't worry. There are some easy, sure-fire steps to success.

Imagine that the assigned topic is "Why Did American Political Leaders Call for a Constitutional Convention in 1787?" Here are the steps for writing a good essay on this topic:

1. **Review what you know.** If your class has already discussed the political ideology behind the Articles of Confederation, the successes and failures of that government, the problems that first constitution of the new nation could solve, and those it could not, then review your notes. Reread the chapters in the textbook that cover this topic, and look once again at any other reading assignments you have been given on these issues and events. Perhaps your instructor has given you a bibliography of books and articles on the subject that will help. Use these materials as resources also.

2. **Develop a thesis, or main argument.** The question being asked is "why?" The answer you develop should focus on motive, circumstances, and precipitating events. For example, your thesis might be: "These political leaders believed that the nation was in danger of total collapse and concluded that the Articles government lacked the powers that were necessary to rescue it."

3. **Write a clear statement of your thesis.** Refer to it as you proceed; don't wander off onto topics or issues that do not reinforce your thesis.

4. **Make an argument that explains and supports your thesis.** Given your thesis, the body of your essay should do the following:

   a. Summarize the powers the Articles of Confederation did give the central government; summarize the powers that were purposely denied the central government. Quote, when necessary, from the document itself. (Note: Most textbooks carry a copy of the Articles, the Declaration of Independence, and the Constitution in their appendices. These documents are also readily available on the Internet.)

b. Give several examples of the results of the limitations placed on the Articles government that created major problems. Devote at least a paragraph to each of these limitations. You could write, for example:

```
This government could not raise taxes and thus
it had to rely on the generosity of the states.
The decision not to allow the government to tax
was based on a fear of creating a new tyrannical
government like the one the nation had just
rebelled against. But the result was that the
government could not pay its debts to its own
citizens or to foreign nations, and it could
not borrow money it needed because of its poor
credit reputation.
```

Here is a second example:

```
The Articles government could not control
interstate trade among the thirteen states.
Each state could set tariffs, or import duties,
on goods coming in from other states; each
state could charge the others for necessary
goods imported from Europe and England. The
result was constant rivalry, exploitation, and
resentment.
```

c. Describe a crisis that might have prompted these political leaders to believe that the nation was on the verge of collapse. For example, you can discuss news of Shays' Rebellion in 1786, a farmers' revolt in New England that set armed citizens against the government of Massachusetts. Men like George Washington feared that anarchy was about to replace law and order in the nation.

5. **Always enliven your essay, where you can, with quotes from the historical figures themselves.** Do you have a letter from George Washington that describes how concerned he was about the nation's growing debt? Do you have a pamphlet or a newspaper article attacking the Articles for their weakness? Often textbooks and other secondary sources will include quotes or documents you can use.

6. **Write a conclusion.** Bring all the examples you have provided together to demonstrate the basis for the belief that the nation was in danger of collapse. You may also want to offer your own interpretation of the crisis. Do you agree with the "founding fathers" that the nation was in danger of collapse?

7. **Reread your essay.** Make sure you are convinced by your own argument. Ask yourself: Have I made my point effectively? Have I offered enough examples? Do I want to say that some concerns expressed by these political leaders were more important than others?

8. **Reread your essay—again.** Check for spelling errors. Check for grammatical errors. Make sure you have provided footnotes for all quotes. Make sure you have cited the sources you have paraphrased or quoted.

9. **Add a bibliography (a listing of the books, articles, and other sources you have used in the preparation of this assignment).** Your instructor may want an "annotated bibliography." In this case, you must provide a few sentences on each source, evaluating its quality and its value to you in writing the paper. For example:

Carol Berkin, *A Brilliant Solution: Inventing the American Constitution.* New York: Harcourt, Fall 2002. This book tells the story of the Constitutional Convention, its conflicts, goals, and concerns about the dangers of putting power in the hands of a central government.

☞ *HELPING HAND*   Make sure you follow the instructor's directions regarding length of your paper, types of sources that must be used, and which citation format you should use for footnotes and bibliography.

☞ *HELPING HAND* In reviews and critiques, follow the advice of the best public speakers: tell the reader or audience what you plan to talk about (your introductory paragraph). Talk about it (the body of your paper), and then recap what you just talked about (your concluding paragraph).

Bulletin Board Discussions

With bulletin boards, professors can organize discussions outside the scheduled class period. Your professor might post a question about the assigned readings and ask you to respond. An assignment could include splitting you into groups of five or six students and asking each group to debate a certain question. This is a good tool for analyzing the readings because you get to ask questions and post your views as you are reading. This process can also help you learn more from each of the readings because your fellow students and the professor may have insights you did not consider on your own.

If your professor wants to assign a bulletin board discussion, she will post a link on the course website. Typically, bulletin boards include a form where you can type in your comments as a new "thread" or as a response to someone else's comment. When you are done typing in these boxes, hit the "Submit" or "OK" button. Your message will be added to the discussion, and the professor or your fellow students can then respond. You will see not only your own message and the professor's response but also comments from the other students. A debate can take place among you, your fellow students, and the professor, and you can respond or ask questions of anyone involved. Be sure to bring the same etiquette to virtual discussions as face-to-face discussions. These messages can also stay up on the website throughout the semester, so you may read the messages at any time.

☞ *HELPING HAND*   If you are asked to write more than a one line response on a website, consider writing it offline in a word processor first. You will get the advantages of spell checking, a less distracting interface, and, most important, a save button that lets you keep a copy of your work safe while you write. Many an articulate answer has been lost when bulletin board webpages close unexpectedly or something goes wrong while submitting your answer. Remember too that even though you are submitting this work through a novel, high-tech interface, the content of your work should be as clearly written and organized as any other official classroom assignment.

RECAP

This chapter gave you tips about writing a journal entry, book review, critical essay, and bulletin board entry.

How Do I Pick a Research Topic and Find Information for It?

- *How do I choose a topic?*
- *How do I choose a note-taking system?*
- *How is research conducted?*
- *What sources should I use?*
- *How do I find sources in the library?*
- *How do I conduct research on the Web?*
- *How do I find historical information in the library and on the Web?*

*T*IPS IN THIS CHAPTER

- Choosing a topic
- Taking notes
- Conducting the research
- Critiquing sources on the Web
- Finding information on the Web
- Downloading information from the Web
- Citing the sources

A research paper assignment can ask you to write five pages or twenty-five pages. Regardless of the size, a few tips will help you complete the assignment with a minimum of trouble.

How Do I Choose a Topic?

The first step in writing any paper is to choose an appropriate, manageable topic. Often, the professor will make this choice easier by providing the topic and narrowing it for you. In this case, your job will be to answer the question posed by the professor.

If you are asked to choose your own topic, you will find that this task involves both emotional and practical considerations. At a very basic level, you need to find a topic that interests you. The semester will be very long if you are struggling to write a research paper about an issue that bores you. Take the time to look through the syllabus, read some of the assignments for the class, and talk to the professor so that you can find a topic that truly engages you. Usually, what makes a topic interesting is finding a question you want to answer. "Why was the fur trade so important to the French in colonial Canada?" "What led to the success of the Haitian revolution?" "How was slave labor organized in the English tobacco colonies?" But enthusiasm and curiosity about a topic are not enough.

In choosing your subject, you will have to use common sense. Can the topic be researched and written about in one semester? Can you find the resources you will need in your school library or on the Internet? In other words, is your topic manageable? You will never be able to write a paper that explains the whole history of America's westward migration and settlement in the nineteenth century, but you can explain how the extension of the railroad system aided the settlement movement, or you can examine the role women played in this migration. Making sure you have the proper resources is the second key to success. You may want to write about the social and political consequences of the Iranian Revolution of 1979, but you might not pursue the idea if your library does not contain enough books and articles on this topic. On the other hand, digital collections have profoundly expanded the possibilities for undergraduate research papers. With your instructor's approval, you might be able do research in otherwise distant library collections offering treasures such as George Washington's original letters, songs and memoirs of former slaves, or images and videos of suffragettes marching on Washington—all without leaving your campus dorm room.

Finding a narrowed-down topic that interests you and making sure that your library has many resources on this topic can be painful, but it is critical. In narrowing the subject, you need to calculate how many points you want to make in the given number of pages. A five-page paper usually involves proving a thesis with four or five pieces of evidence; a twenty-five-page paper also proves a thesis, but here you can use more pieces of evidence and additional sections of background information. For example, the role of the railroad in western expansion could be written in five pages that discuss in brief terms the three or four major ways the railroad facilitated the process economically, socially, and physically. A twenty-five-page paper about this topic could include these same pieces of evidence, but provide personal stories about settlers or government documents about land grants to the railway companies, as well as a number of pages of historical data.

In the example given in Chapter 6 for the critical essay, the question posed was: "Why Did American Political Leaders Call for a Constitutional Convention in 1787?" In a research paper, you can ask the same question, but discuss in more depth the political opinions of the leaders involved and the crises that forced them to revisit the whole debate about what kind of government the new country should have.

You should follow the same format that you used for the essay but provide more historical data as background information. You must also supply primary source material so that you and your reader can gain a better understanding about what the different actors in the story felt and believed. This chapter, and the following one, will cover some of the steps you should take to write a research paper answering this question ("Why did American political leaders call for a constitutional convention in 1787?").

How Do I Choose a Note-Taking System?

Before you start doing the research, you need to think about a note-taking system. Without a system, you will face a disorganized mess on the day you start writing your paper. You will waste precious hours if you wait until the last minute to organize the information you have gathered. You will have trouble figuring out what information is missing and what you may still need to research.

☞ *HELPING HAND* If you start researching a topic and find that the library and the Internet do not have enough information or have too much (i.e., the topic is too broad), you need to alter your topic. This could involve merely changing the focus a little bit or changing the entire topic itself. Talk to your professor and your school librarian; they can help redirect your work.

1. Choosing a note-taking system:
   a. One common system is to use index cards. Write only one piece of information on each card. When you start writing your paper, you have an instant organizational system because you can put all the cards containing similar information in one pile and continue until all the cards are organized.
   b. You can also use an outline system. In this case, you divide the outline into the different sections of your paper and place relevant information under each of your outline headings.

☞ *HELPING HAND* Regardless of the system you choose, you must keep track of where you found each piece of information. Make sure that every card or outline entry includes information about the source, including the page number. You might also want to include the call number of a book or journal you used, in case you have to return to it.

☞ *HELPING HAND* When citing primary sources on the Web, beware of temporary links from search results as these may expire after a few minutes or hours. You may copy a link to a source from your browser address bar, paste it into a footnote in your paper, and then be dismayed when you (or, worse, your professor) can find only a cryptic error message a day later. Although material does sometimes disappear from the Web, usually the problem arises when your source (and the link you used to reference it) was part of a temporary collection of sources gathered in response to your search request. Somewhere in the Web address, you might see the words "temp" or "tmp" or "search," all danger signs that the link may return an error if the server decides it can forget about your question to make space for new search requests. When linking to a primary source online, examine the link carefully for signs of being temporary and search for any button or address labeled as "permanent," "persistent," or shareable. Believe it or not, the Library of Congress, our nation's premier research library, still hides permanent links at the bottom of the HTML source code of the Web page itself.

2. Mastering the note-taking process itself:
   a. Don't rewrite every line in every book you read. This will slow your research and could lead you down the road to plagiarism. (See Chapter 10 for an explanation of plagiarism.)
   b. Write out individual quotes you know you want to use, and make sure that you write the entire quote correctly (or make a photocopy of that page).
   c. For other pieces of information, write in a kind of shorthand. Write down only key words and phrases, not complete sentences.

☞ *HELPING HAND* Make sure that you can understand the words and phrases later. Don't cut corners so much that the notes are worthless on the day you finally sit down to write the paper.

How Is Research Conducted?

Research requires utilizing as many resources as you can find. Begin scouring your school library because it contains primary and secondary books and journals, and possibly even tapes and videos that you can use for your research paper. (See Chapter 5 for a definition of primary and secondary sources.) Don't forget to use the Web, not only for printed sources but also to find people in your neighborhood who have special insights into your topic. Just remember that the best documents are still often hidden from popular search engines and must be located using the specialized search forms of the websites of the Library of Congress and other major research libraries. You need to do the legwork to find as many of the relevant sources as possible.

☞ *HELPING HAND* For almost all research papers, your professor will require that you utilize primary sources. Rarely will a professor assign a research paper without them because they provide the real building-blocks of any historical writing. Your professor wants you to serve as a junior historian, analyzing the raw data for yourself and not relying solely on the words of others.

What Sources Should I Use?

A good rule of thumb is to start with sources containing a broad analysis of your topic and gradually move toward sources with a more focused analysis. What does this rule mean for you? Start with a few secondary sources to get an historical overview of your topic. Once you have a strong understanding of your topic, you can start reading more specialized sources. These will often be primary sources because they give a hands-on narrative and opinion about the events you're describing and analyzing. Don't limit yourself when it comes to primary sources. Personal diaries, government documents, treaties, letters, and published interviews may all be helpful, but you might also find novels and poetry helpful for your analysis because they give alternative views about your subject. In general, it is best to move from the general to the particular, from books that set the broad historical context to books that focus on specific issues or events that relate directly to the question you have raised in your thesis.

☞ *HELPING HAND* Your professor will often require that you use certain types of sources and answer a certain type of question. Make sure you understand the assignment before you start your research so that you won't waste a lot of time looking for the wrong kinds of information.

☞ *HELPING HAND*   While the Web is a wonderful tool for getting information quickly, do not rely on it exclusively when writing a research paper. Push yourself away from the computer screen and go to the library. The best resources will be at the library, both in terms of the written documents stored there and the personal help you will receive. Librarians are in the library to help you; take advantage of their assistance and expertise.

How Do I Find Sources in the Library?

Probably by now, every library in the country has a computer database program that allows you to access the materials. Every database program is slightly different, so you need either to find an instruction sheet somewhere near the computer terminal or to ask a librarian how to use your school's program. Many libraries also allow you to access the database from your home computer. Ask your librarian or computer department for instructions. Your library almost certainly subscribes to scholarly journals and primary source collections in digital form. A librarian or electronic resources specialist can guide you to invaluable collections containing research treasures such as colonial American pamphlets and newspapers, ancient Latin texts, and searchable archives of scholarly journals going back hundreds of years.

All books are not created equal, as the saying goes. The books available range from secondary sources to autobiographies of famous people, to government documents, to novels. For example, the autobiography of a politician involved in a major policy decision will probably provide a very different account of that decision-making process than a scholar who studied it years later. This is why Chapter 5 reminded you that not all secondary sources arrive at the same conclusion, even when the same facts are used. And that's why you can't rely on a single source—or even two or three—to tell your tale in a research paper. Make every effort to find as many different perspectives on your topic as you can.

How Do I Conduct Research on the Web?

The Web literally becomes a more useful source for historical writing every day. You can use it to get a biography of someone, check on that date you need to include in your paper, get a wide range of opinions about a given issue, and so on. Since library books are so expensive, many schools are now asking their students to rely on Web research whenever possible. Even in cases when the library is well stocked, the

Web is now an invaluable source for finding pieces of information that were previously found only in dark and dank archives.

The Web is a completely unregulated medium, however, so any person, in any country, can post information to it. What does this lack of regulation mean for you? Even more than when you do research in the library, you must question the source of *all* the information you obtain on the Web. You must evaluate a Web source just as you do a book, journal, or magazine by making every effort to find out who wrote the piece, who its target audience is likely to be, and what its political slant or opinion is. Without this process of evaluation, you cannot be sure you are using valid data in your paper. Here are some examples of websites that must be evaluated and used with care:

1. Groups like Amnesty International and Human Rights Watch post reports about human rights abuses perpetrated by countries around the world. These reports provide information often unavailable in books, but the reports are also controversial because the countries under examination frequently disagree with the findings. To use these sources, you should always indicate the organization issuing the report and any information you can find about how the data was obtained. For example, the data could have come from interviews with political prisoners or from newspaper reports.

2. As crises develop around the world, more people are writing first-hand accounts and sending them via email or list-serves to those outside the affected area. These insights can be invaluable if they are used correctly, but be careful not to claim that this information is undisputed truth. Provide some background information on the author in your paper and explain that this is a subjective, eyewitness account.

3. Groups like the Ku Klux Klan post their racial views on the Web. You might want to use this kind of source if you're writing about racial politics in America. If you write about this group's views, always indicate the source; do not write as if the majority of people in the country agree with them.

4. Governments, politicians, and political organizations around the world are beginning to use the Web to put forward their opinions. For example, Hezbollah, a military and political organization stationed in southern Lebanon, and the current president of Iran both have specialized websites. These sites contain information and quotes unavailable anywhere else, but here too you should indicate the author of the site and the fact that these organizations and politicians have political motives for getting this information out to the world.

5. Many people—outside the university system and the political world—have posted sites discussing the activities and writings of major historical and literary figures and major historical events. A small number of sites might be of value, but generally the analysis presented is not at a university level and should be avoided. These are amateur sites, so you have no way of guaranteeing the information they contain.

6. News outlets such as CNN and the Associated Press have websites. If you're writing about a contemporary event, these websites can be useful because they often provide articles and reports from many different news sources. However, the very nature of the news industry necessitates that you use these sources with caution. Newspapers and cable stations always want to be the first to publish a piece of information, to "get the scoop" on their competitors. In the rush to get the information to the public, many of the facts may be left out of the story or they may be completely wrong. To avoid this problem, follow the story over a few days, or even a few months, to see how the story evolves over time. Also, try to use a number of different news sources as a way of backing up your own facts. One news source might ignore information that another source uncovered.

☞ *HELPING HAND*   Instead of the old saying "innocent until proven guilty," think in terms of "guilty until proven innocent" when dealing with information on the Web. Initially assume that all the information you find on the Web is questionable. Only after you do the research to find out who the author is and what his or her motivation is for creating the site may you consider using the information obtained.

Although you must use the Web with care, there is no doubt that it has become a great source for all kinds of information, including material that is also available in your own school library. The advantage of the Web in this case is that it makes these sources easier to access. Check the Web for the following:

1. Universities and libraries have posted millions of primary sources to the Web. Among the best are the American Memory project of the Library of Congress, the Victorian Web at Brown University, Yale University's Avalon Project, the New York Public Library, the Gilder Lehrman Collection, and Georgetown University's American Studies Crossroads Project. Each of these collections, and thousands

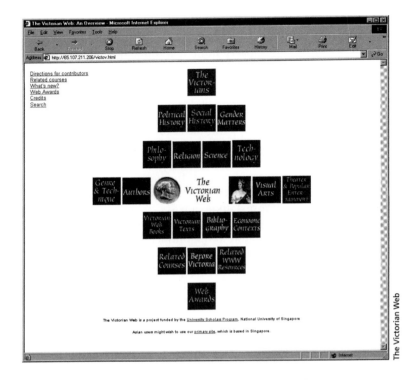

The Victorian Web

more like them, have powerful search engines that draw primary sources from their collections for display directly on the Web. You may use these documents in your paper as you would primary documents you found in the library.

2. Major newspapers and academic and political journals like *The New York Times*, *The Nation*, and *American Historical Review* post articles to the Web. In addition, foreign newspapers, often in English, appear on the Web every day. You may use these as you would the hard copies.

3. Many historical essays and articles have been written by university classes like your own or by professors themselves. In this case, the URL will usually include the identification *.edu* as an indicator. Generally, these sources will be secondary sources because the class and the professor have done their own research, similar to your own. You may quote from the analysis they have included, but you should go to the original sources for the more substantive facts. A

good paper will always cite all the sources and a bibliography, so this search should be an easy process. Think of a page like this as a guide to finding more information.

4. Historical societies and research institutes post historical essays about any number of issues. You may use these sources as secondary sources, but be sure to indicate in your paper the source of the information, and always try to find the original sources of the information obtained.

5. Governments all over the world post parliamentary, congressional, and diplomatic documents to the Web. You may use these as primary documents.

6. International organizations like the United Nations post resolutions and laws on their websites. You may use these sources as you would the hard copies generally available in government depositories.

7. Online encyclopedias have also proliferated on the Web. Wikipedia is by far the most popular and, on average, compares well with traditional encyclopedias for accuracy. University students should use such resources with caution. The analysis presented in them is often at a high school rather than a university level. You may use these sources, but only for simple background information such as names and dates, not for analyses or quotes.

How Do I Find Historical Information in the Library and on the Web?

With the enormous number of sources available to you on the Web and in your library, you may ask yourself, How do I find information quickly and efficiently? It helps to think in terms of peeling an onion. Merely cutting off the skin shows very little of the onion. Layer by layer must be peeled away for the center to appear. In doing research, each layer will provide a different piece of the story. Also some layers are more important than others for a given project.

Layer 1

The best way to start finding information in the library and on the Web is by typing broad phrases into the library catalog, major libraries and archives, or the most popular search engines on the Web—http://www.google.com, http://www.yahoo.com, http://www.bing.com, etc. All of these programs and sites provide a box for typing in the search criteria. As tempting as it is to type your paper topic into the search field of your favorite search engine, first look for major digital primary source collections featuring any of the central actors in your paper—former presidents, many authors, sports heroes, activists, and organizations—at the nation's leading research library websites such as the Library of Congress and the New York Public Library. If you come up empty handed and have to turn to a more general search engine, try adding "Papers of" or "Collection" to any names for which you are searching as that will bring primary source collections to the top of what might otherwise be a very long list of websites, only a few of which will contain useful original documents.

For example, for information about the American Civil War, try each of these methods and compare the results. In your library database, the names of the different books will be shown. At major archives such as the American Memory Project (http://memory.loc.gov) at the Library of Congress, the Valley of the Shadow Project (http://valley.lib.virginia.edu), or Documenting the American South (http://docsouth.unc.edu), type your search phrase in their custom search interface. Then, try a general search engine such as Google in whose search results a short description will appear under each URL. Read them to see which sources are closest to the topic you are actually researching. Also, remember that the search engines rate each of the sites to determine which are more important for this search. Thus, the sites that appear near the top of the screen will probably be more useful, but you cannot take this for granted. These searches are really a hit-or-miss process. For example, asking about the country of Jordan will bring up not only a number of sites about the Hashemite Kingdom of Jordan but many more about the basketball star Michael Jordan.

For the sample research paper, try:

Articles of Confederation
Constitutional Convention
George Washington
James Madison
Alexander Hamilton

If too many sites appear after a broad search, try narrowing down the search parameters. To use the American Civil War example, try typing "Women in the American Civil War" or "Battles in the American Civil War" to bring up sites and book lists more closely related to your particular topic. In other words, the more specific the phrase, the better the response will be from the database and/or the search engine.

For the sample research paper, now try:

Shays' Rebellion
Northwest Ordinances
Federalist Papers
Federalists
Antifederalists
John Dickinson (the man who wrote the initial draft of the Articles
of Confederation)

In the Library   Once you have a list of books in the library, write
down the call numbers of the books you want to see or ask the librarian if there is a way to print out or email to yourself a list of the most
important books.

Google, Inc

On the Web   Most search engines are better for one type of search than for another. Once the search engine has generated a number of sites, enter them by clicking on the URL provided. Searching from page to page on the site can be slow, so look for any internal search engine the site might provide. Usually a "search" button of some kind will be on the top of the page or in a frame to the side. If not, surf around the site to see if one is available on another page. If no search option is available, you will have to surf around the site yourself. If the information you want does not appear quickly, go back to the search engine results and try another Web page.

> ☞ *HELPING HAND*   The Web contains too many pages and options to spend too much time looking on just one site. If the information is not on the first site, move on to another.

Layer 2

Use these initial searches to dig deeper into the resources of both the library and the Web.

In the Library   Once you've located a book through the library catalog, hyperlinks for related topics will appear at the bottom of the page. These are Library of Congress subject headings. Every book in the library is stored by its title and its author, and also by the topics it covers. If you don't find enough books via a search for specific titles, try using different subject headings.

You can also use Boolean phrases to narrow your search. Boolean phrases use words like *and* to tell the computer that you want to find titles that contain only the words that you've stated. Ask your librarian about all the different Boolean options available in your library's database.

Most libraries in the United States use the Library of Congress reference system. In this system, books with similar themes are placed on the same shelves. Once you've found a few books or journals via the computer database, check the whole shelf and section to see if any other useful books are located there.

> ☞ *HELPING HAND*   Once you've found books that are useful, be sure to look at the bibliography at the back of each one. Remember: The authors have already done some of the work for you.

On the Web Once you have found a site that appears useful, look through it to see if the authors suggest more sites on the same topic. For example, a number of sites on the author J. R. R. Tolkien not only give information about his life and books but also recommend other sites to visit. Hyperlinks will be provided to navigate you to the other sites.

☞ *HELPING HAND* The Web can become addictive quickly. It is so easy to use and has so much information to offer. Make sure you do not get mired down, moving from one worthless page to another. Remember that the Web is only useful for a class if it gives you the information you need. Do not surf for hours hoping you'll discover the data somewhere in cyberspace. If the information is hidden too deeply, turn off your computer and head back to the library instead.

For the sample research paper, some good secondary sources would be:

Charles Beard. *An Economic Interpretation of the Constitution*. New York: Free Press, 1986.

Carol Berkin. *A Brilliant Solution: Inventing the American Constitution*. New York: Harcourt, 2002.

Forrest McDonald. *E Pluribus Unum: Formation of the American Republic, 1776-1790*. Boston: Houghton Mifflin, 1965.

Richard B. Morris. *Witnesses at the Creation: Hamilton, Madison, Jay, and the Constitution*. New York: Holt, Rinehart, and Winston, 1985.

Jack Rakove. *Original Meanings: Politics and Ideas in the Making of the Constitution*. New York: Knopf, 1996.

For the sample research paper, some good primary sources would be:

Avalon Project at the Yale Law School, http://www.yale.edu/lawweb/avalon/avalon.htm (Posted to the site are many primary sources surrounding the Articles of Confederation and the U.S. Constitution)

Lyman Butterfield et al., eds. *The Book of Abigail and John: Selected Letters of the Adams Family, 1762–1784* (1975). Cambridge: Harvard University Press, 1975

The Federalist Papers

The Articles of Confederation

The U.S. Constitution

Layer 3

In the last few years, a new type of electronic index has appeared in library databases. It directs users to newspaper and journal articles, as well as to government documents. These are important new tools because the regular database searches do not uncover the same kinds of sources. These indexes will find keywords in articles. For example, a search for Thomas Jefferson in a regular library database will probably list only the books about him. An electronic index will list all articles with his name in the title as well as any articles where his name appears in the body of the text.

The indexes are generally accessible only through a university or college Internet connection. In other words, you must log on to the Web using a school log-in program or access the indexes while at school or from home using your university log-in credentials. Schools must pay for the right to use them, unlike search engines like Google, so only enrolled students may access them. Ask the librarian at your school or check the school's website to find out which indexes you can use. A few examples follow:

JSTOR: This index searches for journal articles and allows the user to download full-text versions of them in different formats.

Lexis-Nexis: This index directs the user to newspaper and journal articles published in the last twenty years. The citations are listed, and many of the articles can be downloaded for free or a small fee. This site is useful for papers covering current events.

Public Affairs Information Service (PAIS): This index provides citation information for books and articles, but it does not provide full-text versions of any of them.

Libraries also collect bibliographical databases, like *Historical Abstracts* and *America: History and Life,* which provide lists of articles and books written about a given subject. Ask your school librarian to see which bibliographical databases your school owns.

Layer 4

Government agencies and departments throughout the country and the world provide copies of the documents they produce.

In the Library   Most large libraries in the country have collections of U.S. government documents. You find these documents by using the library database program. If your library is too small, find out how to gain the right to use a larger one in your area.

On the Web   The U.S. government, as well as many other governments around the world, has increasingly begun to place documents on the Web, which makes them accessible to all users. On many of these, documents, laws, maps, census data, and additional documents may be downloaded to the user's computer.

A good starting point for U.S. government documents is: http://www.firstgov.gov.

Layer 5

Local governments and private individuals have established research centers, tourist sites, museums, and lobbying organizations all over the country. They look at local, national, and international issues, as well as gender, class, and historical items, to mention just a few topics. If you want information from them, write, call, or visit their centers. Most of them now have Web pages so you can easily obtain their contact information. These institutions are often loaded with information that you can't find anywhere else.

Layer 6

The Web has also spawned an enormous number of listservs where you can discuss thousands of different topics, from Revolutionary War battles to environmental concerns. While a lot of junk passes around the various listservs, they do highlight current events and publish articles pertinent to a particular topic. Two different types of listservs appear on the Internet.

1. Some listservs allow you to view a discussion taking place on a given subject from a Web browser. To find one, use a search engine to search for a particular topic. The listserv will appear as a URL; click on it and you will be able to view the most recent discussion. One particularly good website is H-Net: Social Sciences and the Humanities, found at http://www2.h-net.msu.edu.

2. Some listservs require you to sign up to receive the information via email. Again, a search engine will find pages discussing different topics. When you click on a site that states that it has a listserv, look at the instructions on the page.

Typically, you will have to send an email message to the listserv. In the body of the letter, you will have to type a specific line (as instructed on the Web page).

You will then receive dozens, if not hundreds, of letters a day. Remain on the listserv if interesting issues are discussed, but remove yourself from the list (by following the instructions on the Web page) if you do not find it useful. You do not want to waste precious time reading through worthless emails.

Downloading Information from the Web

Most pages have automated the process of downloading information from the Web, but here are two methods for completing this process.

Automated: When downloading an article or file from the Web, check to see if a button or hyperlink labeled "download" appears somewhere on the page. If so, click on it and then follow the directions on the screen. The biggest decision you will have to make will be where the file should be saved. After clicking on the particular "download" button, a box will appear asking for the location of the desired file. Go to the top of the box, to the line that says "Look in:" and click on the down arrow. Search through the folders on the computer until the correct one is open. Then hit "OK" or "Save," depending on which program you are using.

Manual: If the program has not provided a download option, then you must save the file manually. Open up the page you want to save and click on "File" and "Save" or "Save frame" (depending on which program you are using). You will then be prompted to pick a folder in which to save the file. Use the instructions above to find the appropriate folder and then save the file. On some operating systems, such as the Mac OS, you can save a website by "printing" it to a Portable Document Format (PDF). Select the print command in your browser, and then look for either a "Save As . . ." or a simulated printer that makes PDFs. The advantage of these files is that they are faithful facsimiles of the printed version of the page you are viewing.

The files saved by these methods will probably be in an HTML, PDF, or word-processing format. To avoid having to guess the format, the best method is to open the file manager on your computer. In Windows, this will appear as "Windows Explorer" and on the Mac it is called the "Finder." If you are using a different type of operating system, you must search your computer for a similar program.

Once you have opened the file manager, search until you have opened the folder with the appropriate file. Click on the file two times and the computer should open the appropriate program. If it does not, then you will not be able to view the file because you do not have the right kind of program.

Adobe Acrobat Reader Many Web pages have created Adobe Acrobat files to ease the process of reading long, complicated files. For example, the U.S. government uses the Adobe format for almost all of its tax files. Files written in languages that do not use Latin letters (Arabic, Hebrew, Russian, for example) often appear in the Adobe format.

To read these files, you must have the Adobe Acrobat Reader program installed on your computer. This program is free and can be obtained in many different places. The easiest place to look is on the Web page where you want to read an Adobe file. Often the producers of the page will place a button, a hyperlink, somewhere on the page saying something like "Download Adobe Reader Now." If the Web page contains this button, click on it and follow the instructions.

If no hyperlink appears, go to the Adobe Acrobat Reader home page at http://get.adobe.com/reader/ and follow the instructions.

Layer 7

Be creative about choosing your sources; not everything is within the covers of a history book.

Depending on your topic, you can, for example, interview people involved in the events you're describing. If you're writing a paper about migration to the United States, find someone who arrived here via Ellis Island in New York. That could be your very own grandmother!

Or you can utilize photographs or stills from movies and documentaries to enhance your analysis. Jacob Riis took photographs of immigrants in New York City at the end of the nineteenth century. If you were writing that same paper on immigration, you could show his pictures as examples of how the immigrants worked and lived in the city. At the same time, you need to be aware of the fact that Riis often put his subjects into posed positions so that he could represent their lives as he imagined them.

☞ *HELPING HAND* The fact that Jacob Riis rigged some of his photographs to show what he imagined was the truth should remind you that you should always check who the author of a source is, regardless of the type of source. Photographs can display a bias just as easily as a written article.

Fictional sources, such as poems, short stories, and novels, provide a unique glimpse into historical eras. For that same immigration paper, you could quote Emma Lazarus's famous poem, engraved on the Statue of Liberty today. "Give us your tired/your poor. . . . " A novel by Charles Dickens could add flavor to a paper on nineteenth-century working conditions in London.

In other words, use your imagination! These additional sources will improve your research paper and make the whole process more interesting for you.

RECAP

This chapter gave you tips about choosing a research topic and conducting the research. The key to this process is to find a topic that interests you and that can be researched using the resources at your disposal. It also means that you need to use your imagination as you conduct your research. Don't take the easy route; try to find unique sources that bring your topic to life.

8

*H*ow Do I Write a Research Paper?

■ *What is the difference between an analysis and a narrative?*

■ *What steps should I follow when writing my paper?*

What Is the Difference Between an Analysis and a Narrative?

One of the most common problems students encounter when starting to write any kind of paper is recognizing the difference between an analysis and a narrative. An analysis looks at different pieces of evidence and presents a thesis. In other words, an analysis proves a point or answers a question. A narrative describes the event, usually in a chronological manner. A narrative of World War II would look something like this:

In 1939, the German army invaded Poland and thus started World War II. The Germans then conquered the Netherlands and France through its blitzkrieg offense. The United States entered the war after the Japanese attack on Pearl Harbor, on December 7, 1941.

An analysis would answer a question, such as the following:

How did the Germans successfully conquer Poland, the Netherlands, and France?
Why did the United States enter the war?

Most research papers combine analysis and narrative. The problem for the student is to find the right mixture of these two styles. Research papers should always be constructed around an analytical framework, with narrative sections used only to prove the different points.

What Steps Should I Follow When Writing My Paper?

Step 1: Write the Thesis Paragraph

The thesis paragraph is the cornerstone of your paper. You must present your thesis as clearly as possible so that the reader will know the direction you plan to take. The thesis sentence itself—the question you plan to answer—can appear anywhere in the thesis paragraph, but it is most often placed at the beginning or the end of the paragraph. You must also detail the most important points you plan to make in the paper, so that you give the reader a guideline to follow.

☞ *HELPING HAND* The thesis paragraph is so important because it's your chance to tell the professor what you plan to prove in the paper. You have all the power in this situation: you tell the professor exactly what you want to say and the professor checks to see if you've done it effectively.

A thesis paragraph for the question, "Why Did American Political Leaders Call for a Constitutional Convention in 1787?" could look like this:

American political leaders believed that the nation was in danger of total collapse and concluded that the Articles of Confederation government lacked the powers necessary to rescue it. Financial concerns, diplomatic crises, and a farmers' revolt highlighted how weak and ineffective the Articles government had become. These problems confirmed for many of the country's political leaders the need to create a stronger central government, while at the same time recognizing the political rights of the states. The provisions of the U.S. Constitution ultimately reflect the historical context in which they were written because they established the strong central government the country clearly needed at the time, while providing a system of checks and balances to supervise the powers newly granted.

Step 2: Write an Outline for the Whole Paper

Don't start writing immediately; make an outline of the main points you plan to present. Each section of the paper should analyze a different aspect of your paper. In other words, each section of your paper should answer a different aspect of your question.

Organize your notes according to the outline. If you've used note cards, pile them in different areas of the room, depending on where they go in the outline. If they're in the computer, collect them under the relevant outline heading. For the sample research paper, the outline could look like this:

```
I. Introduction (Thesis)
II. Short History of the Revolutionary War and the
     Writing of the Articles of Confederation
   A. Victory in the Revolutionary War
   B. Political Opinions of the Political Leaders
      1. Fear of Creating an Authoritarian
          Government
      2. Power of the States
      3. Different Views of Citizenship, Political
          Rights, Democracy
        a. John Adams
        b. John Dickinson
   C. Provisions of the Articles of Confederation
III. Financial Problems under the Articles of
      Confederation
   A. Postwar Depression
      1. Costs of Rebuilding After the War
      2. Speculators
      3. Destruction of Markets during the War
   B. Problems of Tax Collection
```

C. War Debts Owed by the Articles Government

D. The Articles Government's Inability to Impose Federal Tariffs

E. Economic Problems and the Northwest Ordinances

IV. Diplomatic Crises under the Articles of Confederation

A. British Support for Indian Resistance in the Ohio Valley

B. Spanish Concerns with American Settlers in Mississippi, Kentucky, and Tennessee

C. Barbary Pirates in the Mediterranean

V. Shays' Rebellion

A. Causes of the Rebellion

1. Land Rights Issues

2. Economic Problems in the Postwar Period

3. Inflation

B. "Stay" Laws

C. Failures of the State and Federal Governments

VI. Constitutional Convention

A. Members

B. Political Differences of the Members

1. States' Rights versus the Power of the Central Government

2. Slavery Issues

C. U.S. Constitution

VII. Conclusion (Reiterate the Thesis)

This outline highlights the *reasons why the Articles of Confederation had to be revised*; it does not provide a narrative of events.

Throughout the paper, utilize both primary and secondary sources. Use secondary sources for analysis and primary sources to highlight the real voices of the people concerned with these events. For the sample research paper, the primary sources could include:

The papers of all the political leaders Libraries all over the country and sites now on the Web have collected the writings of just about every major figure involved in writing the Articles of Confederation and the Constitution. Use them throughout your paper to show why these men felt the Articles had failed. If a secondary source gives a quote from, say, James Madison, don't use that source; find the primary source. Use the secondary source only if you can't find the original.

Government documents When writing about a specific document, like the U.S. Constitution, always quote from the original.

Historical sites and museums Cities up and down the East Coast have museums and historical sites designed to highlight the early years of this country's history. Contact them to get additional information for your paper.

☞ *HELPING HAND*   Always keep your thesis in mind while you're organizing the paper so that every part of the outline answers part of your question. If a point in the outline has nothing to do with your thesis, delete it.

Step 3: Write a Rough Draft

The old cliché that claims, "I always write better under pressure," is not true. Actually, you just write under pressure because you know you have a deadline. Papers written the night before the due date generally look like rough drafts and receive much lower grades than they would have if they had been written progressively over a few days. The best option is to write a rough draft a few days before the due date and show it to the professor or to one of your friends. You can then incorporate their suggestions into your final draft. At the same time, this break will allow you to step away from the paper for a couple of days. You can then read the paper over and bring fresh ideas to it.

☞ *HELPING HAND*   Caffeine is not a substitute for a good night's sleep. Don't put yourself in the position of having to "pull an all-nighter," because you will not be able to take the time to write a rough draft, you will not be able to get the advice of your professor, and you will not be able to find grammatical or thematic problems.

Go through your notes, concentrating on one section at a time. Always keep in mind the question you're trying to answer; don't give information that has nothing to do with your thesis. Every paragraph in the paper must add some key piece to the puzzle.

You must cite the sources of your information. See Chapter 11 for tips on citing sources.

When you finish writing the paper, read it through a number of times to check for grammatical errors and to make sure that you successfully proved your point.

☞ *HELPING HAND*   The act of writing generates the process of analysis and might very well make you rethink your ideas about the topic. If you get to the end of the paper and find that your evidence proves a different point than you initially wrote in the thesis, change the thesis.

Step 4: Edit the Final Draft

Once you've shown your paper to your professor or to a friend, make sure you consider all of their suggestions and make the appropriate changes. It's often difficult to identify problems with your own writing; outside readers are invaluable in this process.

☞ *HELPING HAND*   Don't forget to add a bibliography to the end of the paper. The professor needs to know what sources you used. You can't take any shortcuts in this process.

RECAP

This chapter discussed all the steps necessary for writing a research paper. You must utilize several skills in the process, from hunting down the right sources to organizing an analytical paper. You should ask your professor for advice about sources, your topic, and the writing of the paper itself.

CHAPTER

9

*H*ow Do I Join Class Presentation Assignments and Debates Successfully?

- *What is involved in a class presentation?*
- *What is role playing?*
- *What is a class debate?*

Most history assignments involve writing, but many professors like to assign individual or group oral presentations too because they help you hone speaking skills that will serve you well in your future career. Doctors, lawyers, administrators, and real estate brokers, for example, all find themselves standing up in front of a group and presenting data they have collected and analyzed. So think of these class presentations as invaluable opportunities to improve your job prospects after graduation.

What Is Involved in a Class Presentation?

A class presentation involves both preparation and then the actual presentation.

Preparation

The best way to get over the stage fright associated with giving talks in front of a group of people is to come to the class as fully prepared as possible. If you have done your research thoroughly, written a couple of drafts of your talk, put together useful materials for the class, and rehearsed the whole presentation in front of the mirror, a lot of that fear will disappear. In the following section, part of a sample twenty-minute presentation entitled "The Influence of European Imperialism on Africa" will be prepared.

Group Work   If the assignment requires that you work with another person in the class, meet together as soon as possible and divide the workload. The best way to do this is to divide the topic into segments so that each person covers a different theme or a different period of historical time. Ask the professor for advice if you do not know how to divide the work fairly and economically. These assignments can always be changed later as the research brings out new aspects of the topic, but this is a good step because it provides a solid foundation for each section that you will discuss in the final presentation.

In addition, at the first meeting, make a schedule for all future meetings so you can work at a steady pace. Get everyone's phone numbers and email addresses so you can contact each other whenever you need to do so.

☞ *HELPING HAND*   The biggest problem with group work is making sure that everyone carries his or her share of the load. Avoid problems by meeting at regular intervals and supervising each other's work. If one person still does not do enough work, talk to the professor as soon as possible.

Research   Approach the presentation as you would a paper: get the topic from the professor or come up with one of your own (depending on how the assignment is worded in the syllabus), narrow it down, and then find the necessary sources. As early as possible in the semester, consult with the professor about the topic and discuss the sources available at the school.

☞ *HELPING HAND*   Don't wait until the last minute to start the research process. Calculate how much time you think the project should take—and add a bit more for good measure. You don't want to be frantically hunting down sources in the library the night before your presentation is due.

Writing   Until this point, the process has been the same as writing a paper for the class. Now, however, you need to think about the best format for presenting the information orally. Writing a paper and reading it, line by line, for twenty minutes will be boring for you, the professor, and your classmates. To give a successful presentation, you need to find a livelier way to present the information.

Step 1: Make an outline of the major themes you want to present. Since the average student presentation lasts about fifteen to thirty minutes, you should think in terms of having three to six major points to discuss, depending on the assigned time for yours. For the sample presentation, the major points include the following:

```
I. Economic Imperialism
II. Cultural Imperialism
III. Colonial Imperialism
IV. Changes in Africa as a Result of European
    Imperialism.
```

Step 2: Under each of these points, write complete sentences discussing them, either in paragraphs or in an outline form. Paragraphs work well when you want to connect the information in your own mind. This format is closer to writing a normal paper. The outline format saves a little time, but it is helpful only when you already know the key points you want to discuss and do not need to think through your analysis in quite the same way. Samples of both are shown below.

```
I. Economic Imperialism (Paragraph Style)
```

```
European sailors began to trade along the West
African coast at the end of the fifteenth century.
European merchants had traded with Africa for
centuries, but the goods had come across the Sahara
Desert and the Mediterranean Sea. To increase
their profits, the Europeans wanted to find a
more direct way to tap into the ivory and gold
available for sale in Africa. In the last decades
of the fifteenth century, as shipping technology
improved and sailors could explore the West Coast
of Africa, European merchants came along to make
the necessary trading contacts. When they arrived
on the coast, these merchants began to barter
European manufactured goods for the raw materials
available in Africa. During the next century, the
```

Europeans solidified their positions along the coast by building their own trading forts and by making strategic alliances with the different kingdoms trading in the region.

II. Cultural Imperialism (Outline Style)
   A. Catholic and Protestant missionaries arrived in West Africa almost immediately after the sailors first touched on the shore.
   B. From the coast, they quickly worked their way further inland.
   C. In small villages, they set up churches and schools.
   D. As part of the process of converting Africans to Christianity, the missionaries taught European languages and incorporated Africans into their church as workers.
   E. The first converts were Africans who were alienated by their own religious or societal beliefs.
   F. Others converted to obtain jobs with European merchants.

Step 3: After putting together the main points of the topic, you must organize them into a presentation. You do not want to read the paper, line by line. A more natural approach works better for oral presentations. To organize a successful presentation, you now need to put together an outline of key words and phrases. These phrases and words should be descriptive enough to trigger your memory about the larger topics to be presented. Write longer sentences if you need additional clues about the information.

I. Economic Imperialism
   A. Europeans Discovered West Africa in the Fifteenth Century
   B. Changed Trade Routes—Sahara to Coast

C. Traded Ivory and Gold
D. Shipping Technology Improved (This technology allowed the Europeans to sail along the whole coast for the first time.)
E. European Forts Dotted Coastline
F. Europeans Directly Involved in Trade in Africa

☞ *HELPING HAND*   To give a good presentation, you must know your key words and phrases as thoroughly as possible. These words and phrases will mean nothing to you on the day of the presentation if you have not read through the information several times. You must practice your presentation to guarantee that you understand and remember the information.

Step 4: Type out a clear copy of your outline or write the phrases and words on a series of index cards. If you have to fumble through your notes during the presentation, the students and the professor will lose interest. It is very important that you organize the outline or the index cards as efficiently as possible. For example, use different colors and fonts so you can easily distinguish the different topics.

Step 5: In addition to the task of putting together a well-researched presentation, many professors will ask you to provide supplementary materials to highlight the most important aspects of the topic. These supplementary materials could be outlines, maps, images, or even food.

The computer programs discussed below only help you present the information to the class. You should still write the talk itself on a separate outline or on index cards.

Word-Processing Program   If you want the students and the professor to have a broad outline of the topics you plan to discuss, you can type this outline using any word-processing program. To distribute it to the class, print the page and make a copy for everyone or print it out on a transparency.

Economic Imperialism

1. European Discovery of West Africa
2. Trade

3. Technology
4. European Forts

***PowerPoint*®**   You can also use a program called PowerPoint, which creates presentations very easily. The program automatically provides outlines and allows you to insert pictures or images between the lines of text. However, as anyone who has suffered through awkward, haltingly read PowerPoint presentations can attest, the program is no substitute for clear thinking, good writing, and a persuasive and interesting argument. If possible, use your voice to convey your major arguments, handouts for complex documents or information you want your audience to review while you speak, and the relatively small area on the screen for the kind of evidence it communicates most effectively: historical images, color charts, maps, and meaningful interactive models and animations. Do not design your presentation as a series of bullet points on the screen. Grab your audience's attention with well-phrased questions, intriguing mysteries to be solved, and telling evidence. And of course, come prepared with notes and images you can pass around if (for most of us, when) the computer fails just as you are turning to face the class.

Web Page   You may also create your own Web page for a presentation. The advantage of this is that the Web allows you to construct a public document that might prove interesting and useful to a wider audience than just your professor. While a PowerPoint presentation is good for the twenty minutes you are actually speaking, a Web page can be put up on the Internet and the students can reexamine it at any time, twenty-four hours a day, while the semester continues.

Images   Pictures and maps can add a visual image to the topic you are presenting. You can get images by downloading them from the Web or by scanning them into your computer from books. You can then put them into your Web page or PowerPoint presentation or print them out as transparencies or hard copies. See Chapter 13 for instructions about how to perform these functions.

Examples of images to be used in the sample presentation:

Portuguese caravels (ships)
European trading forts
Missionary villages and churches
A map of West Africa
A map showing European exploration routes

Depending on your topic, you might find that other items are important to show to the class. You can prepare or buy food from a given geographical or cultural area. In the sample presentation, you could bring in yams because much of West Africa subsisted on yams. You could also bring in clothing from the region. Try to be creative.

☞ *HELPING HAND*   Even if the professor does not require these additional materials, try to come up with some ideas of your own. Make sure, however, that these materials enhance your presentation. Do not show a lot of pictures just because you can find them; show only those items that help explain your topic.

Step 6: Organize all your cards, transparencies, outlines, and images into the format needed for the presentation.

Step 7: Practice your presentation in front of a friend or a mirror. If you are doing a group project, make sure you practice the whole presentation together. Only by going through a practice-run (or two or three) will you know if the presentation runs for the right length of time and if your trigger words are good enough to allow you to discuss all the information you have put together. In the practice runs, go through your additional material as well to make sure all of it is organized sufficiently.

If you find, after a couple of practice runs, that the phrases and words written on your outline or index cards do not trigger enough information in your mind, change them. Write out longer phrases or add a few more words. The thing to remember is that these cards are your guide. You need to make them as useful as possible. What works for one person will not necessarily work for another. By practicing the talk ahead of time, you can find your own system.

☞ *HELPING HAND*   You may be surprised to know that many professors experience stage fright. So if you are still afraid, even after following all these steps, go to the professor to discuss the problem. He will probably give you tips for overcoming the fear because (1) he wants you to succeed, and (2) chances are he understands the problem all too well.

Presentation

If you have followed the steps listed above, the presentation should go off without a problem. In the end, the key to the presentation itself is practice, practice, practice. If you know your information and your materials well enough, the presentation will be easy. Since things can and often do go wrong with the laptops, projectors, and myriad cables used to give a digital slide show, be sure to have backup notes in paper form so you can still make your presentation without the computer. Save a backup of the presentation on a USB storage key or on the Internet in case you need to use the file on a different computer unexpectedly.

What Is Role Playing?

Role playing involves stepping into the shoes of an historical character and putting voice to his or her words. The reason professors use this device is to encourage students to look closely at the opinions expressed in different countries and by different historical figures. While other assignments certainly serve this function as well, role playing adds a new component to the process. Role playing requires that you speak in someone else's voice, defend another's position. To do this, you must know that person's ideas well enough to uphold them, regardless of your own particular views. You should come away from a role-playing session with a new perspective on how hard it is to negotiate treaties, determine policy decisions, and decide who to support in a given debate, to name only a few instances. Role playing allows you to step inside the mind of an historical figure you have studied merely on paper.

A common role-playing device is to act out a mock session of the United Nations, or another international or regional organization, and have students represent the different countries involved. The professor will typically present the forum with a problem—the status of Northern Ireland or the issue of economic sanctions against Iraq, for example— and ask that the students negotiate and debate as if they were the Prime Minister of England or Saddam Hussein.

Another example of role playing is a military re-enactment. By representing the soldiers who fought at the Battle of Gettysburg, for example, you will better understand how the North won that battle and why geography and the amount of supplies held by each side can easily change the balance of power on the battlefield.

You could be asked to act out a play that may be a work of fiction but that highlights some of the historical themes of the period. An example would be a Shakespearean tragedy. You could also be asked to act the roles of some of the characters involved in European imperialism in Africa, people like an African king, a European missionary, or a European administrator.

How do you study for something like this? As with any assignment, the answer is to complete the homework and do any extra research the professor requires. You will not be able to represent that African king if you do not understand his religious views or the alliances he has possibly made with the new European arrivals. If the information is not included in the regular reading for the class, talk to the professor about the extra research you should conduct.

What Is a Class Debate?

Like role playing, debates require that you defend a particular political or moral position and persuade others to support your side. Debates typically involve two opposing sides—each represented by either one person or a group of people—and a moderator. The moderator asks the questions, and each side then has a specified time to state its positions. After each side has done this, the first group usually gets to respond to the other side's views. The professor will lay out the rules for the debate beforehand so you will understand the format.

A debate can cover just about any issue in history. Some debates might re-enact a political debate, such as the John Kennedy–Richard Nixon debates in the presidential elections of 1960. Others might debate the pros and cons of capitalism and communism; still others might debate the merits of the American Constitution.

The key to success, as always, is to research and study your materials thoroughly because debates delve deeply into the issues. That debate about the American Constitution would cover diverse issues such as states' rights, equality of the individual, and the bases of power in the new state. To be successful, you must do the required readings for the class and then any additional research the professor assigns. Like the presentation and role-playing examples above, you could be asked to take different sides in the debate over whether European imperialism ultimately helped or harmed Africa. Issues in the debate might include economic benefits from increased trade, African dependence on European products, religious benefits from conversion to Christianity, and the loss of indigenous religious traditions.

To prepare for the debate itself:

Step 1: Debates move very quickly, so you do not want to waste time shuffling through your notes. You must prepare a series of index cards or an outline of the key topics to be debated. Regardless of the format you choose (index cards or an outline) do not write long sentences detailing the different positions. Write short phrases or key words that will trigger your memory about the larger pieces of information.

Step 2: The best policy is to follow the practice, practice, practice philosophy. While you might not know every question the moderator plans to ask, you can make a good guess and pretend to answer the questions in front of the mirror. By doing this, you make sure you really understand the issues and that your notes have the right trigger words. If you forget some of the facts, write longer phrases on your notes, to guarantee that they trigger your memory on the day of the debate. If you are working within a group, get the whole group together one or two times to practice the debate together. One person can act as moderator while the others debate the issues.

Step 3: On the day of the debate, get to class a little early to prepare your notes. You might want to bring in a glass of water. Most people get very thirsty while they speak before a group. During the debate, try to look at your audience. People instinctively trust someone who looks them in the eyes (and the goal of a debate is to convince the audience that your position is the correct one). If you get nervous, try to look just at the professor or one of your friends. They want you to succeed just as much as you do. If you start to get nervous or confused, stop and take a look at your notes or index cards. Take another deep breath and give yourself a little time to think about the next piece of information you want to discuss.

☞ *HELPING HAND*   Every in-class presentation gets easier. The stage fright really does diminish each time you successfully complete a presentation.

RECAP

This chapter walked you through all the steps necessary for a successful presentation, debate, and role-playing exercise. The key to success is preparation. You need to conduct the research, prepare any necessary multimedia programs, and practice, practice, practice before you step in front of the class. If you have followed all the advice in this handbook, you'll discover that these kinds of presentations are easy.

What Is Plagiarism and When Would I Be Cheating on My Paper?

- *What is plagiarism?*
- *How can I recognize the different kinds of plagiarism and cheating?*
- *How can I avoid plagiarism?*

TIPS IN THIS CHAPTER

- Definition of plagiarism
- Types of plagiarism and cheating
- Facts

What Is Plagiarism?

Plagiarism is the intellectual theft of someone else's ideas and words. When you plagiarize, you are taking someone else's work and attempting to pass it off as your own. This seems straightforward enough, but when you are writing a research paper you may find yourself saying: "All the information I have collected is new to me. How can I tell what is unique enough that it must be cited?" If you are in doubt, ask yourself the following: Are these words unique to this author? Have I seen this idea anywhere else? Have I really put this into my own words?

■☞ *HELPING HAND*   If you are tempted to plagiarize, consider this: Your professor is not stupid; you will rarely be able to fool her. The reasons? (1) The books and articles you use for your research, and from which you might consider plagiarizing, contain more sophisticated analyses than the average student can produce. As a result, she'll have no trouble spotting material taken from a published article. (2) Your professor reads many more books and articles than most students do, so she might very well recognize the original source immediately. If she does not, she can contact friends in the field who can probably point her in the right direction. (3) Your professor knows how to use Internet search engines as well as her students; she can find the same paper you can. Many colleges now subscribe to plagiarism-fighting databases where thousands, perhaps millions, of papers once offered for sale on the Internet are stored for cross-checking against suspected plagiarism cases.

How Can I Recognize the Different Kinds of Plagiarism and Cheating?

Plagiarism comes in all sizes and colors, sometimes blatant and sometimes more subtle. Several different types of plagiarism are described below.

Word-for-Word Transcription   This example is the easiest to define. Plagiarism rules are very explicit on this point. It is forbidden to copy someone else's work, word for word, and present it as your own. If only one sentence in the paper contains a word-for-word transcription, the paper is plagiarized. Word-for-word transcriptions must be placed within quotation marks and the source cited.

Unique Terms   Authors often invent their own terms to make a given point. These invented words or phrases are often combinations of two words or a merger of an English word and a foreign one. Sometimes, the word has been given a new definition by the author. Frequently, the word or combination will be contained within quotes. If you do not see this term in another article or book, you can assume that it is unique to the author. You must cite the source of any such terms.

Paraphrasing   A common misconception is that if you change a few words in a text, the text is now your own. This is not true.

- If you copy the same basic sentence structure as the original text, you are plagiarizing, regardless of how many nouns and verbs you change.
- If you present your evidence in the same order as the original text, you are plagiarizing.

In other words, if you retain the same stylistic and analytical framework of the original text, you are plagiarizing.

Despite these potential pitfalls, paraphrasing can be part of your paper. You may begin a section of paraphrasing by saying something like, "Author X states . . . " or "To paraphrase author X's work . . . " and then provide a citation at the end of the section.

☞ *HELPING HAND*   The best way to avoid crossing the line into plagiarism is to work solely from your own notes and your own interpretations of the data and not directly from the book.

Papers on the Web   Thousands of websites selling and giving away prewritten papers have been created in the past decade. Without any doubt, it is plagiarism to copy or buy a paper from the Internet and present it as your own work.

Papers Written by Your Friends   Fraternities, sororities, campus organizations, and your own friends often keep old papers on file.

Copying these papers represents plagiarism because you did not do the work and the words are not your own.

Papers You Wrote for Another Class   Many students have an interest in a particular topic or region of the world and so they take a number of courses covering it. As a result, students may find themselves writing papers on similar subjects. You are cheating if you submit a paper to more than one class.

Citing Works You Have Never Read or Data You Haven't Collected   The following group of offenses are loosely connected and constitute cheating.

- Padding your bibliography with materials you have never read.
- Changing the results of your data to better fit your thesis.
- Citing a source you did not actually consult.

▐☞ *HELPING HAND*   If you're not sure if a piece of information should be cited, ask the professor. If the professor isn't available, err on the side of caution and cite the source. It's always better to use too many citations than too few.

How Can I Avoid Plagiarism?

Several options for avoiding plagiarism are available to you. Some of these options are described below.

1. Conduct sufficient research to have an understanding of what material is unique to a particular author and what information is not. This sounds like a heavy burden, but this is the goal of a research paper—to find enough information to present your case and to prove your thesis.

With each source you find, you'll have a better understanding about what information is unique to a particular author. If you do a shoddy research job, your paper will not be good, even if you don't plagiarize.

2. Never write your paper with a book or an article open in your lap or propped up on the desk. Always take notes while reading your sources, placing the ideas and facts into your own words. Only exact quotes should be written word for word and, in those cases, you should place quotes around the passage and indicate the source of the quotation. If you try to take a shortcut and highlight your sources with a marker, you're setting the stage for plagiarism later. It's much too tempting to use the original author's words if the book is right in front of you. If you write out notes in your own words from the very beginning, you're working from your own statements, not the original author's.

When you start to write the paper, place all the original sources (the books, the articles, whatever you've used) away from the computer or your writing pad. You should work only from your notes. At this point, your job is to write sentences and paragraphs that best present your analysis of the various pieces of information you've compiled. You are now reworking and rewriting your notes, not the original author's.

3. Don't copy and paste information from the Web. The procedure for copying text from a Web page and pasting it into a document is so easy that you may be tempted to do so. *This is plagiarism.* Students cannot take a section of someone else's work and pass it in to a professor as their own. Plagiarism rules apply to the Web as stringently as they do to traditional sources found in books, journals, and magazines. Quotes and pieces of information may be taken from Web pages but the sources must be properly identified in the paper.

This information is so important that it needs to be repeated: *Do not be lulled by how easy it is to get information from the Web; copying and pasting someone else's words constitutes plagiarism.*

The Web should be considered a tool for research, just as a book or a magazine has always been. The Web offers thousands of newspapers, analyses, and critiques that can add to the quality of a student's paper; but only as the stepping-stones to a good paper, not as the body of that paper.

☞ *HELPING HAND* Professors have access to the same websites as the students. This means that professors can easily surf the Web and find the sources when they suspect plagiarism has occurred.

After reading about all these problems, you may be asking yourself, when can I use the copy and paste function on the Web? Since the Web can be considered a source for research, it is acceptable to copy and paste small pieces of text from the Web into a document of research notes. Next to the text, the URL of the Web page, the writer of the text (if identifiable on the page), and the date the text was obtained should all be included. In the final paper, the text must then be cited in a footnote or endnote to identify it as someone else's words and ideas.

☞ *HELPING HAND*   If you do not heed the advice offered in this chapter, your professor and your school administration will bring you before an academic conduct board. Every school in the country has a clearly stated plagiarism policy that may differ slightly from the wording presented in this book but that covers the same general issues. The punishments for plagiarism include probation, suspension, and expulsion from the college or university.

RECAP

This chapter illustrated the many types of plagiarism so that you can avoid the pitfalls they present. Plagiarism is a serious offense because stealing intellectual property is the same as stealing a stereo. School is a time for you to learn how to think and how to write. If you steal the work of others, you're destroying the benefits of your own school experience.

*W*hat Information Do I Have to Cite?

- *What kind of information must be cited?*

- *What kind of information does not have to be cited?*

- *What citation system should I use?*

- *What information must be included in footnotes, endnotes, parenthetical citations, and bibliographies?*

- *What is the proper form for the second citation of any source?*

- *How do I cite websites in my paper?*

- Information to be cited
- Information that does not need to be cited
- Citation styles

To grade your paper, your professor will, among other things, look to see if you've used good quality sources to support your thesis. The citations you place throughout the paper and the bibliography you supply at the end provide that information. Think of these sources as the building blocks of your entire paper. Your professor needs to know what sources were primary and which were secondary, when they were published, who published them, and so on. You need to investigate your sources before you use them (as described in Chapter 5), and your professor will do the same when you turn in your paper. In that way, the professor can determine if some sources are better for your particular topic than others, and if you've used a sufficient number of sources to construct your thesis.

Two issues present themselves when you think about citing sources in your paper:

1. What information do I cite?
2. What citation system should I use?

What Kind of Information Must Be Cited?

The following list describes several kinds of information that must be cited in a scholarly work, including your research papers.

1. **Quotes.** By citing quotes, you're acknowledging the uniqueness of people's words.
2. **Ideas, analyses, and opinions.** Identifying a unique idea, analysis, or opinion is probably the hardest aspect of deciding what to cite. The goal of most authors is to present a unique analysis of a given event. Your job is to find that analysis and to acknowledge that it is "owned" by the original author. Here are some guidelines.

- Every paper you read will have a thesis, often presented in the first or second paragraph. The thesis of a book usually appears in the introductory chapter. You must cite the source of this thesis.
- If you read an analysis in one source that does not appear in any other, you must cite the source of that idea.
- A good rule is to cite any statement that includes objective terms such as "he believed," "she felt," or "they thought," because only the original author can voice such an opinion.

3. **Unique words or phrases created by the author.** Often, historians create new words to express a given phenomenon because they don't feel that regular vocabulary words truly articulate their ideas. Cite any words or phrases that seems a little strange to you because they're used in a unique way or if they seem to be a combination of two or more words.

4. **Disputed facts.** If you encounter a debate about a given date, then cite the different sources and explain, in your paper, why the date is disputed. If historians question the facts of a given event, you must cite the source you choose to use.

5. **Paraphrasing.** *Paraphrasing, without citation, is plagiarism.* You may not copy the bulk of a sentence or paragraph, change a word or two, and present it as your own work. For that matter, you can't change a few words and present it as your own work. As long as you retain the basic structure and ideas of the sentence or the paragraph, it doesn't matter how many words you change; you are still stealing someone else's work if you don't include a citation. You *may* paraphrase another author's words if you identify the author, by stating his name in the text and by citing his work at the end of the passage.

☞ *HELPING HAND*   Since plagiarism rules often vary at different colleges and universities, the best course of action is to ask your professor whenever you're confused about citing sources.

What Kind of Information Does Not Have to Be Cited?

1. Generally, you do not have to provide a citation for a date.
2. Generally, information you find in your textbooks can be considered "common knowledge" and so it does not need to be cited.
3. Many analyses that appear in your sources can be considered "common knowledge" because historians do not question them. These analyses could include statements such as "The U.S. anti-war movement grew during the course of the Vietnam War" and "The nineteenth century witnessed an explosion in railway building throughout the world."
4. Avoid citing every sentence in a given paragraph. You can state near the beginning of the paragraph that you will be discussing a person's words and then you can put one citation at the end of the paragraph.
5. You don't have to cite your own words. You shouldn't be afraid to present your own analyses in a paper. Students often feel that they have to rely solely on the historians' works they find printed in books or on the Web. Use that information to construct your own thesis.

What Citation System Should I Use?

Various citation systems have been devised, the most familiar being the *Chicago Manual of Style* and the *MLA Handbook for Writers of Research Papers (MLA)*. Ask your professor which system she prefers. Your options include footnotes, endnotes, or parenthetical citations. If the professor does not have a preference, choose the system you want. You must also include a full bibliography at the end of each paper, unless otherwise directed by the professor.

☞ *HELPING HAND* Regardless of the citation system you choose, be consistent. Do not use parenthetical citations for half the paper and footnotes for the second half. Do not use the Chicago system sometimes and the MLA system at other times.

This handbook is too small to discuss in detail all the different citation styles. Only a general overview will be provided. For an exact list of citations, buy the Chicago Manual or the MLA guide, or access either one on the Web.

What Information Must Be Included in Footnotes, Endnotes, Parenthetical Citations, and Bibliographies?

In both systems (Chicago and MLA), depending on the type of source, you must include the following kinds of information.

Books
Author(s) of the book
Title of the book
City of publication
Publisher
Date of publication

Here is an example of a footnote or endnote in the Chicago system:

[1]Adam Hochschild, *King Leopold's Ghost: A Story of Greed, Terror, and Heroism in Colonial Africa* (Boston: Houghton Mifflin Co., 1999), 125.

The MLA system recommends the parenthetical style for documentation. An example of a parenthetical note in the MLA system is shown here:

(Hochschild 202)

An example of a bibliographic entry in both the Chicago and MLA systems appears as shown here:

Hochschild, Adam. *King Leopold's Ghost: A Story of Greed, Terror, and Heroism in Colonial Africa.* Boston: Houghton Mifflin Co., 1999.

Edited Volumes
Editor(s) of the book
Title of the book
City of publication
Publisher
Date of publication

If you are citing a chapter in an edited volume, you must also cite:

Author(s)
Title of the chapter

An example of a footnote or endnote in the Chicago system is shown here:

¹Ainslee Embree, "Imperialism and Decolonization," in *The Columbia History of the 20th Century*, ed. Richard W. Bulliet (New York: Columbia University Press, 1998), 150.

The MLA system recommends the parenthetical style for documentation, an example of which is shown below:

(Embree 150)

The following is an example of a bibliographic entry in the Chicago system:

Embree, Ainslee. "Imperialism and Decolonization." In *The Columbia History of the 20th Century*, edited by Richard W. Bulliet. New York: Columbia University Press, 1998.

The following is an example of a bibliographic entry in the MLA system:

Embree, Ainslee. "Imperialism and Decolonization." *The Columbia History of the 20th Century*. Ed. Richard W. Bulliet. New York: Columbia University Press, 1998, 147–171.

Journal Articles
Author(s)
Title of article
Title of journal
Publication information (volume number, date of publication)
Page numbers

Here is an example of a footnote or endnote in the Chicago system:

[1]Samira Aghacy, "Lebanese Women's Fiction:
Urban Identity and the Tyranny of the Past,"
International Journal of Middle East Studies 33,
no. 4 (November 2001): 505.

And this is an example of the parenthetical style recommended by the MLA system:

(Aghacy 505)

Here is an example of a bibliographic entry in the Chicago system:

Aghacy, Samira. "Lebanese Women's Fiction:
  Urban Identity and the Tyranny of the Past."
  International Journal of Middle East Studies 33,
  no. 4 (November 2001): 503–523.

This is an example of a bibliographic entry in the MLA system:

Aghacy, Samira. "Lebanese Women's Fiction:
  Urban Identity and the Tyranny of the Past."
  International Journal of Middle East Studies 33:
  4 (November 2001): 503–523.

What Is the Proper Form for the Second Citation of Any Source?

You do not need to provide a full citation every time you cite the same source. A number of different styles can be used when you cite the same source more than once.

1. You can provide a shortened version of the citation by writing the author's last name and the page number, or the author's last name, a shortened version of the title, and the page number. (The latter style should be used if you use more than one source from the same author.)
2. Another shortened version of the citation is created by writing "Ibid.," followed by the page number. This style should be used if you are citing from the same source two times in a row, but from two different pages.

How Do I Cite Websites in My Paper?

You must cite the source of any information you find on the Web. The various citation styles (such as *Chicago* and *MLA*) have slightly different forms, but all require the same basic information. Always include in both a bibliographical and citation note the following information:

- Author/editor
- Title of the Web page
- Publication date and/or the date you retrieved the page from the Web (because pages change so rapidly, you need to indicate the date when you found the information)
- URL
- Include any other information pertinent to that particular article/page, for example, the volume number, issue number, etc.

The *Chicago Manual of Style* has not yet clarified a system for citing websites, so use the *MLA* system for parenthetical citations:

```
(Victorian Web)
```

An example of a bibliographic entry in the *MLA* system would appear as follows:

```
Victorian Web. Ed. George Landow. 1994.
   Brown University. 1 May 2010 <http://www.
   victorianweb.org/>.
```

☞ *HELPING HAND*   Always provide enough information so that your readers can find the website again. It is particularly important that you type the correct (and complete) URL and the date when you accessed the site. Be sure to check the URL a day or so after you first visited the site to be sure you can locate the item again. Many sites highlight a short, permanent URL for each of their pages that might differ from the URL that brought you to there after typing in search words or navigating through sets of similar documents.

RECAP

This chapter outlined some of the occasions when you must cite the sources in your papers and provided you with a short style guide outlining how the citations should actually be written.

12

This Isn't English Class, So Why Do I Have to Correct My Grammar?

■ *Why is grammar important?*
■ *What are the most common grammatical errors?*

*T*IPS IN THIS CHAPTER

- Keep a good grammar book by your side
- Avoid common mistakes
- Edit carefully

Why Is Grammar Important?

A famous historian is fond of recounting the day a student raised his hand and asked, "Do grammar count?" Without skipping a beat, the professor replied, "Yes, grammar do." Why do all professors agree that grammar counts? Because grammar is a tool for communication. It helps writers express themselves clearly and it helps readers follow what is being said. It eliminates barriers to understanding between the two. So that often-asked question, "Why do I have to correct my grammar?" really translates into "Why do I have to worry about being understood?"

If you were stranded on a desert island, a good guide to grammar and proper writing style would still be a necessity. Fortunately, many good guides are available. The style guides most commonly recommended by college professors include *The Chicago Manual of Style* and the *MLA Handbook for Writers of Research Papers (MLA)*. Keep the guide you choose handy, along with a thesaurus and a dictionary. All three are essential tools in academic life.

What Are the Most Common Grammatical Errors?

Here is a list of do's and don'ts, including some of the most common grammatical errors and problems of style. This list is by no means exhaustive. But if you avoid these errors and stylistic mistakes, you will have made a lot of headway toward writing a history exam or paper that communicates well.

1. **Avoid the passive tense.** Make the subject of your sentence a "doer" not someone or something "done to." Good narrative is propelled along, not dragged behind. Instead of "The repeal of the Corn Laws was discussed in the nineteenth century" you will want to write "The British Parliament discussed the repeal of the Corn Laws in the nineteenth century."

2. **Don't leave those participles dangling.** How do you know if you have dangled a participle? That's easy: insert the phrase immediately after the subject of your sentence. For example, test the sentence "Walking across the field, a rock stuck in Joe's shoe" by putting the dependent clause directly after the subject: "A rock, walking across the field, stuck in Joe's shoe." Can a rock actually walk? Shouldn't the sentence say: "Walking across the field, Joe got a rock stuck in his shoe"? Or take another example: "If handled properly, you should be able to pass this exam easily." Do you really need to be handled properly—or does the exam? "If handled properly, the exam should be easy to pass."

3. **Don't split those infinitives.** An infinitive, as in "to sit," "to read," "to go," should not be divided by the insertion of another form of speech.

   Right: I had to sit quickly or I would be forced to stand for the whole trip.

   Wrong: I had to quickly sit or I would be forced to stand for the whole trip.

4. **Make certain the noun and the verb agree.** Singular noun, singular verb; plural noun, plural verb.

   Right: The Constitution and the Declaration of Independence *are* fundamental documents in American history.

   Wrong: The kings and queens of England *is* important figures in history.

   Right: The fall of Rome *is* a major historical event.

   Wrong: Some Americans *comes* from southern Europe.

5. **Do not fall into the habit of calling a country "they."** If you use a pronoun to describe a country, use a singular pronoun, not a plural one. If you discuss the officials in a given country, then you can use the plural pronoun. (And, by the way, a country is not a "she.")

   Right: Egypt *is* a country containing a Muslim majority and a Christian minority. As a result, *it* must be tolerant of both Muslim and Christian laws.

   Right: The leaders in a democratic nation know *they* must answer to the people through regular elections.

6. **Don't shift point of view.**

   Wrong: *We* all want to study history because *you* can apply the skills you learn in other subjects.

   Right: We all want to study history because *we* can apply the skills *we* learn in other subjects.

7. **Make certain each sentence is a complete sentence, not a phrase.**

   Wrong: Lincoln had many goals as president. *Especially to preserve the union.*

   The first sentence is a sentence; the second is a phrase without a subject or a verb.

   Right: Lincoln had many goals as president. He was especially eager to preserve the union.

8. **Don't construct a sentence that is really several sentences combined.**

   Wrong: Louis XIV of France was a proud man he thought he was above the law.

   There are two sentences here, pretending to be one.

   Right: Louis XIV of France was a proud man. He thought he was above the law.

   Or you could create one sentence.

   Right: Louis XIV of France was a proud man who thought he was above the law.

9. **Don't shift tenses suddenly.**

   If you choose to write in the present tense, stick with the present tense. Don't confuse your readers by shifting to the past tense.

   Wrong: Some colonists *want* to rebel. Other colonists *did* not.

   Right: Some colonists want to rebel. Other colonists *do* not.

10. **Have you used the correct word?**

    a. *There* refers to location; *their* means in the possession of several people; *they're* means "they are."
    b. *Its* is a possessive pronoun; *It's* is a contraction of "it is."
    c. *Your* is a possessive pronoun; *you're* is a contraction of "you are."
    d. *Lie* means "to recline"; *lay* means "to put" or "to place."
    e. *To* is a preposition; *too* means "also" or "excessively."
    f. "Ain't" isn't correct in formal written English.
    g. To "affect" something is to have an impact on it; an "effect" is the result of an action taken.

11. Don't end a sentence with a preposition.

Wrong: He had a lot of problems to contend with.

Right: He had to contend with a lot of problems.

☞ *HELPING HAND*　Never sit down to write without a good dictionary by your side. If you are a terrible speller, look for one of those
dictionaries that enter the word in several of the most commonly
misspelled forms and then give you the proper spelling. Most computer word-processing programs alert you to a misspelled word and
then offer you the chance to correct your mistake.

---

12. Use your apostrophes properly.

Don't confuse plurals with possessives. Plurals don't require apostrophes; possessives do.

Right: The queen's robe is elegant.

Wrong: The queen's of England were powerful.

13. You're repeating yourself.

   a. "The reason is because" really translates to "the reason is the reason"; instead, write "the reason is that."

   b. "Revert back" really means "go back back" because *revert* means
   "to go back."

14. Pronouns need nouns.

A pronoun takes the place of a noun. For example, Mary took a
history test. *She* made an "A" on *it. She* stands for Mary; *it* stands
for the history test. But if you start a new paragraph in your test
or essay or paper, you can't start it with a pronoun. The pronoun
needs an antecedent, or a noun that comes in an earlier sentence. So
a paragraph that begins with "He" is like a ship lost at sea.

15. Here is a short list of the most common mistakes.

   a. Don't write "a revolution is when"; *when* signals time.

   b. Don't write "a revolution is where"; *where* signals a location.

   c. Don't confuse "woman"—one female person—with "women"—
   two or more female persons.

   d. Don't write "between you and I"; write "between you and me"
   because "you and me" are the objects of the preposition, not the
   subject of the sentence.

   e. Don't confuse "who" and "whom." *Who* is the subjective case;
   whom is the objective case.

Right: Halt! Who goes there?

Right: To whom are you speaking?

Wrong: To who is that addressed?

Wrong: Whom is the new president?

Is your head spinning? Don't worry. There are scores of excellent grammar books available, some of them with a good sense of humor and most of them inexpensive.

RECAP

This chapter pointed out that writing is a form of communication. To communicate well, you must master a set of grammatical rules that are not designed to torment you or trick you but to help you say what you mean, say it clearly, and say it with some grace and style. Fortunately, you can find several books that set out the rules of grammar for you—clearly and gracefully.

13

*H*ow Do I Make Computer Technology Work for Me? How Do I Succeed in an Online Class?

- *What are the technical issues?*
- *What is netiquette?*
- *What are my professor's virtual office hours?*
- *Can I use images from the Web in papers and presentations?*
- *What must I know to succeed in an online class?*

Computer technology brings exciting new tools into the classroom. It helps you and your professor interact more easily, and it allows both of you to present materials in a multimedia format. But computer technology changes on an almost daily basis, and *The History Handbook* can't cover all the different programs that exist or those that will come into existence while you are reading this book! What this chapter can do, however, is give you some tips on how to use this new technology in general terms that apply across many different programs.

What Are the Technical Issues?

Most courses now have websites hosted by their college campuses. These Learning Management Systems (LMS) include Blackboard®, WebCT®, and a variety of proprietary campus courseware systems. Although these have become a mainstay of campus life, they are not infallible. If you have technical problems, you should let the professor know right away. Other students may be having the same problems, and the professor will be able to work with all of you to resolve them. If the problems continue, he may want to reschedule your assignment. Like you, the professor is mastering new computer technologies and experimenting with their usefulness. He may not be certain which ones will actually help in the classroom, so your input will be invaluable.

What Is Netiquette?

Email and social networking services like Twitter, Facebook, and instant messaging have certainly changed the way professors and students communicate with each other; professors can easily send out messages to the entire class and students can ask quick questions without checking for the professor's office hours.

However, virtual communication should not be considered a substitute for personal interaction between the professor and the student. Email, for example, allows for quick statements and answers, not in-depth debates. Questions concerning problems in the class or drafts of papers, or anything that requires a discussion between the professor and the student, should take place in the professor's office.

☞ *HELPING HAND*   Professors have entered this profession in part because they like to work with students and hear their opinions of the world around them. Thus, students who take the time to visit their professors during scheduled office hours to talk about the class will generally receive a better reception than those who choose to ask their questions only through email.

☞ *HELPING HAND*   When writing an email to a professor, check your spelling and grammar. Email will never be part of the final grade, but a poorly spelled or worded email gives a bad impression of your writing abilities.

What Are My Professor's Virtual Office Hours?

A number of professors are starting to hold virtual office hours (meaning that you can contact the professor via the computer, not in his or her office) in addition to or in contrast to regular, in-the-office hours. As with regular office hours, this is the time the professor sets aside every week to talk virtually to students. Respect that time and contact the professor accordingly. Otherwise, the professor might be away from the computer and will not be able to answer your questions immediately.

Can I Use Images from the Web in Presentations and Papers?

Many professors now require that students prepare multimedia presentations and papers for their classes. These assignments not only enhance your knowledge of the class topics but also prepare you for similar presentations that you might have to give in a future job.

You can find images and maps on the World Wide Web and in books. However, the rules of copyright apply to these images, just as plagiarism laws apply to the text.

Unless otherwise indicated (and some Web pages do say that images in a particular area are free), assume that all images seen on the Web or printed in books are owned by someone.

Class work falls under the "fair-use" policies followed by most colleges and universities. If you are showing an image one time in a class or adding it to a research paper, you usually can do so without obtaining the copyright. Make sure you indicate the source for the image, just as you would cite any quote in the text. Also, check with the professor to see what rules your specific college or university follows concerning copyright.

What Must I Know to Succeed in an Online Class?

With daily improvements in computer technology, colleges and universities are moving toward virtual classrooms, where professors and students interact via the computer and not in person. This type of distance learning is a wonderful opportunity that did not exist just a few years ago. To get the most of this type of class takes a little bit of organizational skill on your part. For one thing, the relationship between the professor and the student changes. In some ways, the connection is stronger because your email lets you spend more time in one-on-one contact with the professor. But emails sometimes don't convey all the feelings and concerns that you can express when you talk them out, face-to-face. A classroom is a much better setting for that. Because of the realities of the online connection, you need to schedule your time carefully and you need to go the extra mile to maintain contact with your professor, both face-to-face and in writing.

While all online classes are designed differently, a few tips can help you succeed. The following paragraphs describe some tips for success in an online class.

Keep in Contact with the Professor   Even though the course is online, try to visit the professor in his office at the beginning of the semester and if you need help throughout the semester. If you meet the professor, he will then be able to attach a face to any emails, papers, and tests he receives from you. This personal contact will be invaluable when he sits down to determine your final grade.

If you live too far away from the school to visit the professor, consider calling him to talk about the requirements for the course at the beginning of the semester. Maintain this contact throughout the semester if you need further explanations about the coursework. If telephone contact isn't possible, email the professor whenever you have a problem or if you want to discuss any of the topics posed in the class in more detail.

Follow the Rules of Email Etiquette When Contacting Your Professor Since email will be your primary contact with the professor all semester, remember that a kind, well-written email will receive a much warmer response than a rude, poorly written one. You will never be graded on your email etiquette directly, but you make an impression with the professor every time you contact him, and he will carry that impression with him as he calculates your grade.

Make Sure You Have Access to the Right Computer Technology If you are using a home computer, make sure it has all the programs required by the online course. You can get a list of the programs from your university or your professor. Also, make sure that your connection is fast enough and stable enough that you won't find yourself unable to access videos, audio, or large documents.

If you need to use a public computer, make sure you can get access to it during class periods and then for long periods of time when class assignments are due. Check with your school's computer office to find out what rights you have to use the computers. Ask about time limits and printing quotas.

Follow All the Instructions Given by the Professor Just like any course assignment, make sure you read the instructions. For example, if the professor tells you to utilize a certain kind of source in a paper, use it. Read the exam questions carefully to make sure that you have answered them properly.

The fact that you're taking the course online presents you with new ways of scheduling your time. Frequently, professors will give you online tests. If that's the case, remember that you are probably being timed. If you take too much time, the program might shut down. Also be aware that once you send your test (probably by hitting a "Submit" button), you will not be able to retrieve the test. Always make sure that you understand all the instructions before you start taking an online test.

Stick to All the Deadlines You should not think of deadlines as only those associated with papers and exams. Online classes have virtual office hours and virtual class periods. You must attend all of them, even though you are sitting at home at your computer. At the beginning of the semester, write a schedule of all the deadlines and display it prominently on your desk. Passing in an assignment late for an online class or being absent from a virtual class session will incur the same penalties as those for a regular class.

Discipline Yourself to Do the Work   Students in regular classes have the professor in front of them two, three, or four times a week as a reminder that they have work to do. For at least that time period, the students have very few distractions. At home, you do not have the same luxury. You need to find a place as far away from any distractions as possible. You also need to allot a certain number of hours every week to your class work. You should not try to get the work done between other jobs. You should make an actual schedule to guarantee that you work, for example, every Monday and Wednesday, from 1:00 to 3:00, on the online class work.

An Online Course Does Not Mean You Should Avoid Campus Completely   Just because the course is online doesn't mean that all the information you'll need will be on the Web. If the course requires that you conduct research, do not focus just on the Web. Follow all the rules laid out in Chapter 7 on conducting research: go to the library, interview relevant people, find photographs, etc. The online course allows you to schedule only some of the class time; consider yourself a regular student for all the other assignments during the semester.

If you absolutely can't get to campus, investigate what libraries and archives exist in your own town. You can then utilize both library and online research for any papers you need to write.

Make Arrangements with Your Professor for the Return of Any Materials   The best way to arrange for the return of your materials is to send a self-addressed stamped envelope to the professor with any work assignments. If the professor has set up a system whereby you pass in every assignment via email or the Web, send the self-addressed stamped envelope separately or drop it off in the professor's office. Most professors don't have a budget for sending papers and tests to everyone in a class.

RECAP

This chapter outlined the most common uses of computer technology in the classroom. You can communicate with your professor online, take images from the Web for your papers and presentations, and even use your computer as the primary access point for your courses. The key to remember is that computer elements should be used intelligently to enhance your class work.

Are There Any Other Tips I Should Know?

- *Why should I go to class?*
- *How can I contact my professor?*
- *How can I avoid problems in this class?*

- Attending class
- Contacting the professor
- Solving problems

Why Should I Go to Class?

Professors are frustrated when students don't come to class, and then arrive at the end of the semester to complain about the heavy workload or ask for an extension. Professors will generally be more responsive to students they know and see on a regular basis.

How Can I Contact My Professor?

Email and the Web provide several ways to communicate with the professor, but they do not replace the professor. If you have a question about a lecture, a paper, or an assignment, try to see the professor during her office hours or make a special appointment.

If you have a question or a problem, discuss it with the professor immediately. Don't let the problem fester until the end of the semester, when you either do badly on an assignment or have to ask for an extension.

How Can I Avoid Problems in This Class?

Keep up with the work; do not leave everything until the night before the paper is due or the exam is scheduled. Do *not* go by the old adage, "I do better when I'm under pressure. I can't write a paper until the night before it's due." If you cram at the last moment, you will not do well. You need to attend class regularly, complete all the readings and assignments, and keep reviewing all your notes.

RECAP

This chapter examined the important relationship between you and your professor. To do well in class, you must attend each class session and, if you have a problem or a question, you should seek out the professor for help.

Glossary

bulletin boards   Provide a means for online communication between professors and students. If a professor has set up a bulletin board, then go to the designated Web page and type or copy and paste the information you wish to send. At the bottom of the page will be a "Submit" button. Hit the "Refresh" button in the menu button to see your entry.

button   Used on Web pages to indicate a hyperlink. You can identify a hyperlink by placing the mouse arrow on top of the button. If the mouse arrow changes to a hand, then the hyperlink will take you to a new area of the site.

cartographer   A person who makes maps.

chat rooms   Instantaneous discussion areas on the Web. Once you access the Web page, you can type your message, submit it, and see it appear on the screen automatically. Other people in the chat room may then respond to you just as quickly.

copyright   The legal right to intellectual property or a creative work. Someone owns the right to every page on the Web. You may not sell or benefit financially from images or maps you retrieve from the Web. Generally, you may use an image or map from the Web in a class, but you must always indicate the source.

cursor   The flashing line indicating where text can be inserted on a computer screen. The mouse can also be used to move the cursor to desired areas of the document.

database The organization of information into fields. An address database, for example, would have fields for first name, last name, street address, town, state, and zip code. To access the database, search for a person's last name or a street address. Many historical websites are supported by databases that you can search for a particular historical event or figure.

download Copying an image, map, or piece of text found on the Web and saving it to your computer. For a PC, place the mouse on top of an image and click the right button. A menu will appear asking you if you want to download or copy the image. Follow the menus on the screen. For a Mac, hold the mouse button down until a similar menu appears. To download or save a piece of text, hit the File and then Save commands on the menu bar at the top of the screen. Sometimes the Web page will give instructions for downloading a file or a program. Follow these instructions when they are available.

electronic index Indexes, like the Social Sciences Citation Index, that can be accessed on your own library database via the Web. Check your school library to see what the URL is for the Web page and follow the instructions. While library databases generally direct you only to books or journals, indexes are more specialized and can provide information about articles and book reviews. Often, these indexes focus on a particular subject, like American history or the history of science.

folder All computers place programs and files into different folders, which organize the data.

HTML A computer language that tells the browser to center a picture, for example, or place a hyperlink on a specific word.

hyperlink   Used on Web pages to allow the user to travel from one page on the Internet to another. Hyperlinks frequently appear as underlined text on the screen or as buttons. When the mouse is moved over a hyperlink, its symbol changes from an arrow to a hand.

icon   Small pictures and buttons on the Web and in computer programs.

Internet   The whole network of computers that connect your home computer to the world. The Internet works something like a telephone network: you dial into your university computer and it routes your request to the appropriate computer.

LCD projector   The device used to project Web pages from your computer to a large screen.

listserv   A list of a group of people who would like to receive email about a given subject. To add your email address to a given list, you must subscribe to it. This usually involves sending a blank email to a designated address. From that point, you will receive all the email sent to that list and may send your email to the entire list as well.

Mac (Macintosh)   A computer that uses the Macintosh operating system.

menu   At the top of most computer programs appears a list of commands, for example, "File," "Edit," etc. Click on any of them with the mouse and a menu will appear with more choices.

operating system (OS)   Every computer has an operating system running behind the scenes to allow users to turn on the computer and access the different programs saved onto it. PCs generally use Microsoft Windows; Macs use their own system.

personal computer (PC)   A computer that uses the Microsoft Windows operating system.

plagiarism   The intellectual theft of someone else's ideas and words. When you plagiarize, you are taking someone else's work and attempting to pass it off as your own.

PowerPoint®   A program that creates presentations on the computer. The program already has a series of templates, so all you need to do is fit your images and text into the boxes provided. You can then display your presentation to a group using a laptop computer and an LCD projector.

primary source   A document or artifact from the historical period under study.

scanner   A machine that "scans," or enters, images and text into your computer.

search engines   Allow you to ask questions on the Web. Examples include Yahoo! and Google. Pose your question by typing in a word or a phrase about your topic and the search engine generates a list of Web pages where you will find that word or phrase.

secondary source   A document or artifact created after the historical period under study has passed.

URL   An address for a Web page and every Web page has one. You may use a URL to access a Web page by typing it into the box provided at the top of the browser and hitting "Enter."

Web browser   A gateway to the Web. Some common Web browsers are Firefox and Internet Explorer.

Web page   The Web is comprised of millions of pages of text and images. Each individual page that appears on your screen is called a Web page.

word-processing programs   Programs that allow you to type letters and papers. The two most common are Microsoft Word and Corel WordPerfect.

World Wide Web (the Web)   The whole collection of pages people have posted to the Internet.

Index